METROPOLITAN LINE

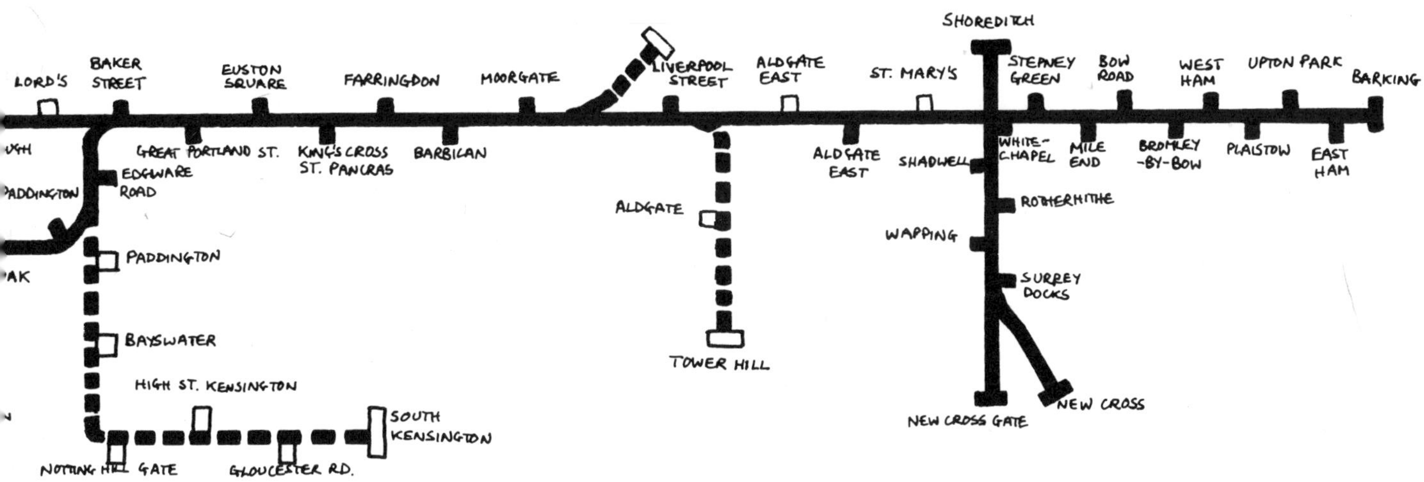

DISTRICT LINE

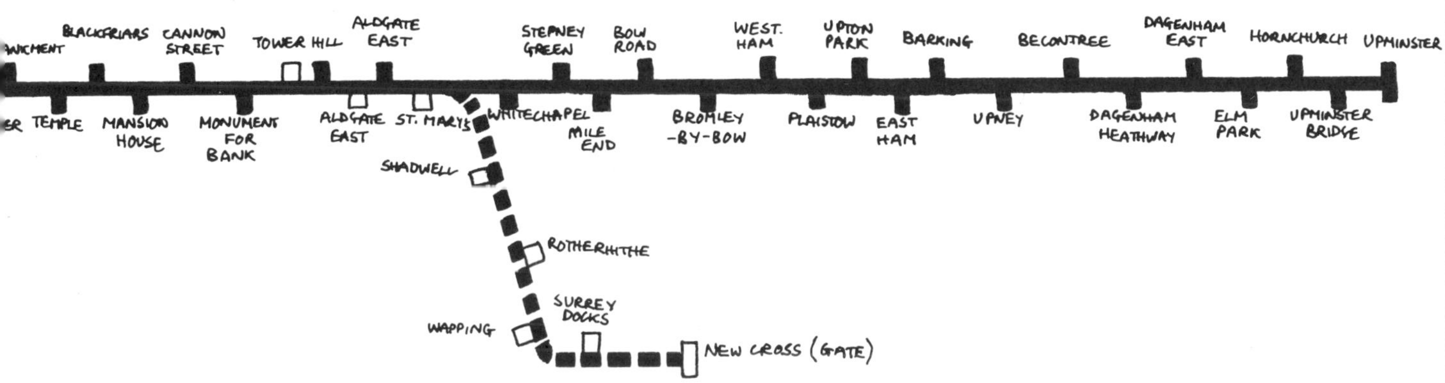

NORTHERN LINE

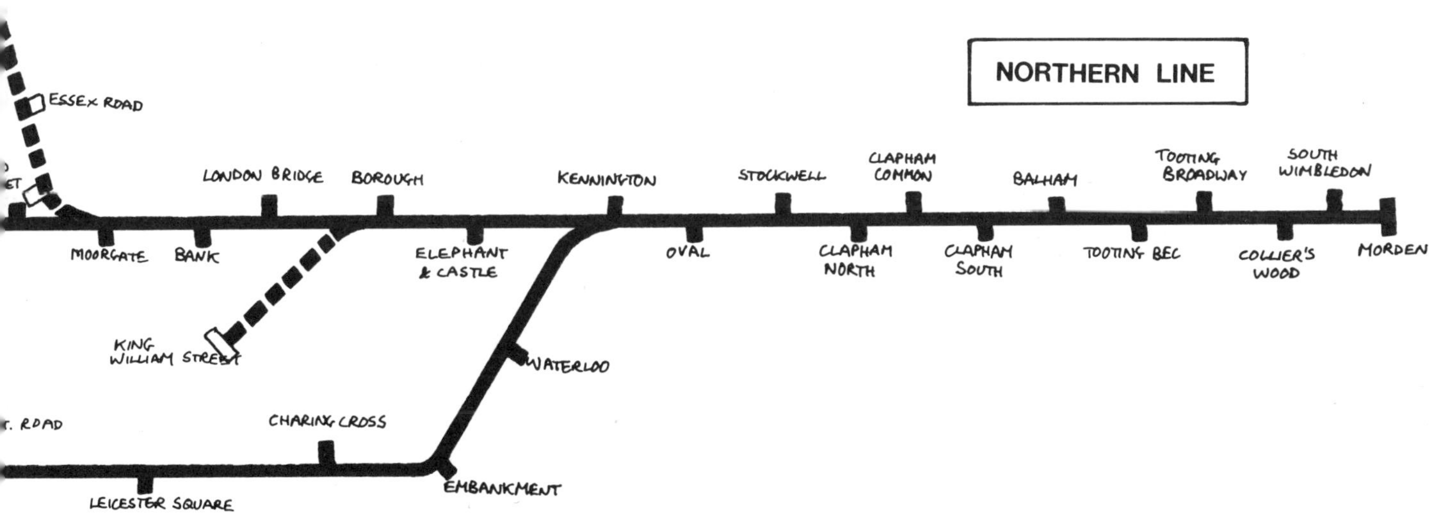

LONDON'S UNDERGROUND STATIONS

A Social and Architectural Study

Written and illustrated by
Laurence Menear

Baton Transport

To M.S.

Also in this series
Metro Memories
Romance of Metro-Land
The Golden Years of the Metropolitan Railway (third of the Metro-land trilogy)
The Final Link (a pictorial history of the GW and GC Joint Line)
Down the Line to Dover
Down the Line to Hastings
Midland Line Memories
The Routemaster Bus

First published in 1983 by Midas Books

Reprinted 1985 by
BATON TRANSPORT
1 Russell Chambers
Covent Garden
London, WC2E 8AA

ISBN 0 85936 124 1

Printed in Great Britain by
Robert Hartnoll [1985] Ltd
Bodmin, Cornwall

Acknowledgements

Of all the people who have helped or encouraged me I should like to give a special mention to the staff of the LT Photographic Library, the RIBA Library and the LT Museum & Library at Covent Garden (particularly Oliver Green, the curator, who read the first draft and made some helpful suggestions). Important assistance was also provided by staff of the LT Department of Architecture & Design and its library. Finally I offer special thanks to the staff of the Underground for putting up with me, and to my mother, who typed it all and corrected my spelling at the same time.

Contents

	Preface	4
	Introduction	5
1	Early Metropolitan and District Railway Stations	7
2	The Advent of the Tubes	33
3	The Evolution of Corporate Identity	52
4	The 'Classic Years' and Beyond	73
5	The New Works Programme and Post-War Developments	93
6	Recent Developments and the Future	114
	Appendix: Logos and Motifs	131
	Bibliography and Source List	133
	Index to Stations	135
	General Index	143

Preface

I have not written this book as either an architectural critic or a railway historian. It was inspired by a general curiosity concerning the differences between stations on the Underground in London, and the project first materialized for a thesis which I produced in my final year of the Illustration course at Harrow College of Higher Education in 1980-1. A few of the drawings date from this time, but most of them were done specifically for this book. Almost all show the stations as they appeared between 1980 and 1983, though a few are depicted as they were many years ago. Although I studied a substantial amount of written material, the nature of the subject involved a great deal of first-hand reference, the result being a book very much related to London Transport's architectural heritage in the 1980s. I have tried at least to mention every station related to the Underground, so that where space precludes a detailed description the reader may deduce a particular station's relevance. There have not, as far as I am aware, been any previous publications dealing comprehensively with the history of architecture and design of London's Underground stations. It therefore seems fitting that I am now completing it in the fiftieth anniversary year of London Transport, 120 years after the opening of the world's first underground railway in 1863.

LJM
March 1983

Introduction

London is unique. This appears to be an obvious fact, but what is it that gives London its own special character? There are so many different aspects to choose from, each of which is just a part of London's identity. The famous buildings, the Thames, the Londoners themselves – these are perhaps some of the special features of London. The transport system has an integral role for commuters, tourists and shoppers. Throughout the world the red bus is as much a symbol of London as the yellow cab is in New York. And alongside the bus in London we find the Underground. Taken largely for granted, it has been London's workhorse for well over a century, and has developed in tandem with the growth of the city. Spanning the decades from the boom years of Victorian railways through to the present day, the system is now as vital to London as it has ever been.

With such a long history it is inevitable that the Underground has contributed greatly to the appearance of London. Underground routes have, to some extent, dictated the growth pattern during this century. Most Londoners live within easy reach of an Underground station, but few probably take much notice of it. It is a tribute to the designers and planners that the system blends in so well, for everybody knows what an Underground station looks like. Or do they? How could one describe an Underground station? They're built of brick and concrete. They've got red tiles on the outside. They're large white stone buildings. They're built below the surface. They're like any other country station. After 120 years it is only natural that they have assumed many different appearances.

The London Underground as we know it today consists of a legacy of privately owned lines which have since been added to and refined. It is only fifty years since the last independent company was brought under common ownership, and it stands to reason that, despite various reconstruction programmes, there are still many types and designs to be seen. Indeed, a Railway Gazette publication of 1946 entitled *Improving London's Transport* noted that 'No railway system in the world offers a greater variety of station types'.

The Underground has been associated with about 330 different stations, including those closed or resited. No two stations are exactly alike in every detail, but in the central area there are family resemblances between the old stations of the independent lines. The Bakerloo, Northern (Charing Cross branch) and Piccadilly Lines offer the most striking example, for all their early stations were built by the same company. Further out, as the system spreads into the suburbs, there is a greater mixture of types. Here one finds the radical new designs of the 1920s and 1930s alongside Victorian and Edwardian country stations and recent additions to the network; each, has its own history and character.

The history of the Underground is one of perpetual adaptation to the changing demands of the capital. In following the chronological development of London's Underground stations we can also gain an insight into both the growth of London and the evolution of design over the last century.

Direction sign at Covent Garden

1 Early Metropolitan and District Railway Stations

The traveller emerging from Baker Street station will find that it is part of a grand building situated on the corner of Baker Street and Marylebone Road, separated from the latter by a long wall. Walking round to the front of this wall he will find a plaque commemorating the rebuilding of the station, dated 24 July 1912 and laid by the chairman of the Metropolitan Railway, Lord Aberconway. Below it there is a smaller plaque erected by London Transport fifty-one years later and unveiled on 24 May 1963. It reads:

Beneath this roadway runs the world's first underground passenger railway. It was opened for public traffic by the Metropolitan Railway Company on 10 January 1863.

This 'roadway' is the Marylebone Road, which together with Euston Road, King's Cross Road and Farringdon Road forms a major route across London from Paddington to the City. The Metropolitan Railway was built to follow this route, and involved seven stations. These were Paddington (Bishops Road), Edgware Road, Baker Street, Portland Road, Gower Street, King's Cross and Farringdon Street.

A glance at a map of London will show that the route of this first stretch of Metropolitan Railway is not wholly within the City, the West End or the governmental district of Westminster, so some background should perhaps be given to explain its existence on the periphery of Central London.

The growth of London began to gather speed in the eighteenth century, and a northern route across town from Paddington to the City was built in 1756. Being a new thoroughfare it was called, logically enough, the 'New Road'. This formed a barrier to the main line railway companies north of the river, which were instructed to build their termini along it. The Great Western, London & Birmingham and Great Northern ran as far as Paddington, Euston and King's Cross respectively, the latter being completed in 1852.

The restrictions of building space and financial considerations ruled out schemes for a central station to link all the lines coming into London. Charles Pearson (solicitor to the City Corporation) had suggested Holborn as the site of this station, but as an alternative a Bill was introduced in Parliament in 1853 for a 'North Metropolitan Railway' to run beneath the New Road from King's Cross to the Edgware Road. Although authorized, the scheme was not a very popular one, the public being shocked by the idea of a wholly underground railway. The necessary backing was not forthcoming until the Great Western, feeling at a disadvantage with its competitors further east, agreed to subscribe the new railway on the condition that it should be extended to run from Paddington through to the City. An amended Bill was passed in 1854 to allow this but further financial troubles (particularly due to the Crimean War) meant that it was a further five years before Pearson's efforts were rewarded. The City Corporation, hoping that goods traffic on the railway would ease street congestion, put up the sum of £200,000 needed for work to begin.

The new railway was built by a method known as 'cut and cover', which involved the digging of a trench down to what was to be track level. This excavation was then covered over with a roof that finished flush with the original ground level. After deliberation it was decided that as the railway followed the route of the New Road this would have to be dug up. The resulting nuisance to traffic was considered preferable to the demolition of buildings along the side of the road. With typical Victorian bravado the road was ripped open, and by the end of 1862 the whole process was completed.

The engineer to the line was John (later Sir John) Fowler, who was also responsible for the new stations. None of these has survived in original form, but all (with the exception of the original King's

Baker Street Original Metropolitan Railway station buildings of 1863 such as this survived with little alteration for many years before an extensive rebuilding programme

Cross) are still in use by both the Metropolitan and the Circle Lines we know today. When constructed, these stations fell into two groups. The two at each end of the line were in open cutting, with a glass roof over the platforms. The platforms at Baker Street, Portland Road and Gower Street were different, for these were the first real 'underground' stations. They were isolated by a shallow, brick-arched ceiling which stretched between the retaining walls of the cutting. Spherical gas lamps hung down to illuminate the chambers thus formed, with the retaining arches along either side continued up to provide daylight shafts. Portland Road (now Great Portland Street) and Gower Street (now Euston Square) are still served by these original platfoms as well as Baker Street, which has grown from being one of the most humble stations to one of the largest and most important Underground stations in London.

The surface buildings on the new railway varied in size and importance, but were generally faced in white stone with arched entrances and windows with balustrading. At Paddington the railway was grafted on to Brunel's station, but at Edgware Road, Baker Street and Gower Street simple buildings were used, the last two each having matching street-level entrances. The building at Portland Road was part of the same family, but the entrance was extended proud of the building and flanked by two domes. Although the eastern terminus at Farringdon Street was larger, the pride of the line was King's Cross. Here the retaining walls of the platform cutting were continued up past street level and topped with a massive semi-elliptical arched glass roof, which ran the length of the station. From the outside the station therefore looked like a huge hall with a curved roof.

When the passenger service was inaugurated in January 1863, there were celebrations, including a banquet at Farringdon Street, and in accordance with the Metropolitan's main line connections rolling stock was provided by the Great Western. This continued for a short time until arguments between the Great Western and the Metropolitan arose concerning the number of trains in use. The projected extension eastwards from Farringdon Street to Moorgate Street caused further friction when the Great Western claimed it had not been allotted enough shares. At short notice the company quit working the line, and the Metropolitan had to call on the Great Northern to take over in August 1863 while plans were advanced for its own locomotives.

The extension to Moorgate Street was completed by 1865, both this station and Aldersgate Street (now Barbican) being opened two days before Christmas of that year. Neither station remains as built, but the layout of Aldersgate Street deserves further comment. The side and central island platforms remain, with four tracks serving them. Short, flat canopies now cover parts of the platforms, but rising above them on either side of the tracks (running below and perpendicular to the road) are the original high brick retaining walls. Set into these are the now redundant brackets that once supported the ribs of a great

curved iron and glass roof, which spanned the whole station. In common with most stations of the time, the platforms were originally wooden-decked. The extra platforms were provided for the 'Widened Lines', opened in 1866 on the south side, and were intended to be worked by other companies. Recently these have been electrified with overhead cables (also running through Farringdon) for an all-electric British Rail service, but at one stage six different companies served the station.

The booking hall and station building, built of light brick with closely spaced arched windows, disappeared along with the roof when they were demolished in 1955. This event was sufficient to move John Betjeman to write his 'Monody on the Death of Aldersgate Street Station'. Today the entrance is through a plain red-brick building, the former glory of the station having been swept away then, and the name was changed to 'Barbican' in 1968.

By an Act of 1864 the Metropolitan was granted powers to extend its line from Paddington to South Kensington, with new stations at South Kensington, Brompton (Gloucester Road), High Street Kensington, Notting Hill Gate, Bayswater and Paddington (Praed Street). The original Paddington (Bishops Road) remained connected to the GWR station, but the new one was placed separately. The line opened in 1868.

Bayswater station is shown here in both its original and present forms. It is the only station on this stretch of line that still exemplifies the original style of the Metropolitan Railway station. Apart from surface ornament the façade of the building looks much as it did when built. In common with its contemporaries it is faced with white bricks. Although the balustrade has now gone, the bases of the urns can just be made out standing proud from the general line of the parapet. Inside, the station has both its two platforms on either side of the tracks, and the high elliptical iron and glass roof so typical of these stations, which were built in cuttings.

The extension itself provided what is probably the most curious piece of architecture on the Underground. In Leinster Gardens, near Bayswater station, two dummy houses (numbers 23 and 24) were built. The railway runs just below them, and they have neither foundations nor substance. The elegant frontage of the houses, complete with painted windows, was erected to preserve continuity of the street's appearance, and thereby also property values. The 'houses' are still there today, a constant source of amusement to those who

Bayswater One of Fowler's second generation stations, this has only undergone minor alterations since it was built in 1868. The insert shows its original appearance, with balustrading and standard canopy

FEATURES OF EARLY STATIONS

Roof and platforms, Notting Hill Gate The roof at Notting Hill Gate is one of the few almost complete examples of its type remaining. Much of the tunnel in the background was built over when the line was later electrified, covering former open sections. Decorative ironwork marking the end of the roof has also disappeared

After the design problems of the various initial Metropolitan stations, John Fowler devised a station type that would normally be built in open cutting, between strong retaining walls. Between the stations were short lengths of covered way, to allow free dispersion of the fumes given off by the steam engines. Uniform features were developed for each station, the most noticeable of which was a high curved roof, with covered gaps to allow steam to escape. These roofs were supported by great cast iron ribs bracketed to the walls. Even at stations where the roof has since disappeared – for example, at Barbican or Sloane Square – it is possible to still see the brackets in place. The East London Railway, which opened in stages between 1869 and 1876, did not have platforms covered with such roofs, but did run in a combination of tunnels and cuttings in the manner of Fowler's Metropolitan & District Railways.

The design of Fowler's 'second generation' stations did much to relieve the noxious atmosphere on the Inner Circle. The worst stretch to travel on was between King's Cross and Edgware Road, where the almost completely enclosed stations and tunnels resulted in a choking mixture of gases. There were, however, those who claimed that this was the best section to visit, for it was rumoured that deep breathing along here was a marvellous cure for all manner of chest and respiratory complaints! Such a visit was surely likely to induce precisely the opposite effect.

Canopy bracket, Paddington At all stations that at some time had a curved roof one can still see supporting brackets in place, such as this example at Paddington on the Inner Circle

Interior of Bayswater Behind the main building and above the platform cutting at Bayswater is a footbridge over the tracks, which acts as entrance and exit to the booking hall. This view shows how the curved roof is grafted on to the brickwork, which has now been painted over

East London Railway platforms, Whitechapel This view, looking northwards towards Shoreditch, shows a scene that has now largely disappeared from the Inner Circle. The cutting has hardly been built over; this would also have been the sort of view one would have expected from Fowler's stations. The platforms date from 1876

Gloucester Road This building, like Bayswater, is a survivor dating from 1868, though its ornament and appearance was later modified. It is adjacent to the later Piccadilly station

have been let into the secret.

Another station that has changed less than most is the Metropolitan and District building at Gloucester Road. It was built in the same style as Bayswater, but with an upper storey. When finished in 1868 the upper floor windows were matched below with high arched entrances in the brickwork. A canopy similar to the old one at Bayswater jutted out over the central entrance to the booking office and a balustrade ran around the top. There was at first a long signboard near the top which read 'Metropolitan & Met. District Railways, Gloucester Road Station, Brompton'. When the balustrade was removed the sign was replaced with the one that remains today, with the names of the railway companies and station picked out in white on a green patchwork mosaic. All the ground floor arches were squared off, and today the station is entered from the side portion, the main building being occupied by shops.

These new extension stations had more in common with those of the new Metropolitan District railway than the earliest Metropolitan stations, where a problem had arisen with ventilation. The system was worked by steam, and the most satisfactory method of locomotive traction that could be arranged involved condensing exhaust steam in enlarged side tanks and releasing it at intervals when running in the open. As the earlier Metropolitan had run almost entirely directly under the New Road (later called Marylebone Road), Euston Road, King's Cross Road and Farringdon Road, the only ventilation at stations was by the staircases. Alterations had to be made at the first batch of stations almost immediately to relieve the pollution of the atmosphere by carbonic acid and carbonic oxide gases. Lighting was, of course, entirely by gas, which did not help the situation. When coal as a fuel was substituted for coke extra openings and blow-holes had to be made in the covered way between Edgware Road and King's Cross. Despite this, the railway had been a success and a new batch of proposals had been laid before Parliament. From these emerged the Metropolitan District Railway, granted powers in 1864.

The new scheme provided for a line to run initially from South Kensington to Westminster Bridge, linked at the former to the Metropolitan. If work was successful, the engineer John Fowler believed, an 'Inner Circle' could eventually be formed, worked by the two companies. The Metropolitan had a large share in promoting the newcomer, and its chairman and three other directors were on the board.

The District began operations in December 1868, just two months after the Metropolitan's stretch of line from Paddington to South Kensington was opened.

Fowler had observed the design error of the first section of the Metropolitan, and determined on more efficient ventilation. He designed the standard type of station, such as Bayswater, to be constructed in open cutting wherever possible. The track was to be laid between two retaining walls, built to different thicknesses if station buildings or other structures were to be built over it. He was responsible for the standard wrought iron and glass roof, and the use of the White Suffolk bricks with Portland cement ornamentation which typified the station exteriors. The stations of the Metropolitan extension and those of the District at Sloane Square, Victoria, St James's Park and Westminster Bridge had a common appearance. Fowler set entrance and exit stairs into the widened retaining walls as well as the station inspector's room and other offices.

Both Victoria and Westminster Bridge had their station buildings nearer the centre of the platforms. The latter had just a plain pent roof over each platform as extra reinforcemement, the proximity of the river making it inadvisable to fit the standard elliptical roof. As with other stations, there has been subsequent girdering over the platforms as new buildings were put up around them. The most noteworthy alterations in connection with this at Westminster Bridge (the 'Bridge' was not omitted until 1907)

Blackfriars This extravagant building was the pride of the District Railway when it was opened in 1870; it sustained severe bomb damage during the last war. The insert depicts its appearance today

Putney Bridge & Hurlingham Built in 1880, this station is now called 'Putney Bridge', but it is here depicted in its 1902 incarnation with the 'Hurlingham' suffix

occurred in the early 1900s with the extension of New Scotland Yard designed by Norman Shaw, RA. The new buildings over the station were linked to it at the east end by a subway to allow, if necessary, a rapid deployment of policemen into the station without bringing them into the street. In 1898 a temporary entrance constructed of timber was opened to the Embankment itself. The redesigning of this was to prove a turning point much later (see Chapter 3).

An extension of the District eastwards was opened in 1870, with new stations at Charing Cross (now Embankment), Temple and Blackfriars. It was built into the new Victoria Embankment and each station was therefore sited next to the new roadway by the river (see the feature on 'Embankment'). The surface entrances were small, with enclosed platforms just below ground level, except at Blackfriars. Here the original platform roof has been extensively rebuilt because of the problems involved in carrying the London, Chatham & Dover Railway directly across it. However, it is not this but its external appearance that distinguished Blackfriars from the other stations.

The District Railway station at Blackfriars had a unique street elevation. The main building was four storeys high, flanked by two towers. The whole was covered in elaborate Moorish-style decoration and railings. One could be forgiven for thinking that it resembled a mosque rather than a railway station, yet here it was in the middle of London next to Blackfriars Bridge over the River Thames. Unfortunately, the ornate superstructure was largely destroyed during the Second World War, and the insert shows the building today, sadly neglected.

Through trains on the District now ran from Blackfriars to West Brompton, completed the previous year. This was another standard station, which remains almost as built except for the paint over the exterior bricks. The roof covers part of the platform and is angled rather than curved. In 1871 the first Earl's Court station, entered by a modest timber building on the east side of Earl's Court Road, was opened. In the same year the District's eastern terminus was opened at Mansion House. This consisted of an unremarkable five-floored building to be sub-let as a restaurant, with part of the ground floor laid out as a booking hall with an entrance on the corner. The building remains today but the corner entrance was modernized in the 1920s, giving it an appearance similar to that of the stations on the Morden line (see Chapter 3).

In 1875-6 the Metropolitan pushed on past Moorgate Street to a temporary Liverpool Street Station, replaced within six months by Bishopsgate (now Liverpool Street) and Aldgate, leaving a gap in the Inner Circle. Interest in the project was declining because of a feud between the Metropolitan and District Companies, as a result of which each began extension programmes away from the joint project.

Rotherhithe One of the original East London Railway stations of 1869 which were taken over by Metropolitan and District services in 1884. Recently the interior has been rebuilt, but the external appearance is unchanged

The Metropolitan was already working a line from Paddington (Bishops Road) to Hammersmith, which had been promoted by a separate company, the Hammersmith & City Railway. Although the line was worked for nearly a year from June 1864 by the Great Western between Hammersmith and Farringdon Street, the Metropolitan took over responsibility in 1865. The line was entirely in the open, and served the red-brick Great Western stations at Royal Oak and Westbourne Park from 1871 and 1866 respectively, as well as others built for the new line at Notting Hill (now Ladbroke Grove), Latimer Road, Shepherd's Bush and Hammersmith.

Platform construction at Latimer Road was largely of timber, and the outlines of the planking can be seen through the tarmac covering. Similar stations were opened much later, in 1914, at Goldhawk Road and a replacement Shepherd's Bush. Between these a station called Wood Lane was built in 1908. It was later called White City, and finally closed in 1959. Hammersmith station was resited in 1868, and further work was done on it between 1939 and 1948.

In 1868 the first steps had been taken on the north-west extension to the Metropolitan. New stations at St John's Wood Road, Marlborough Road and Swiss Cottage had been opened, all built with the brick arches and balustrading of their contemporaries.

The District struck out westward to North End (Fulham, now renamed West Kensington) and Hammersmith in 1874. Hammersmith was destroyed by fire in 1882 and rebuilt in seven months. The District continued over London & South Western Railway tracks in 1877, coming to serve Shaftesbury Road (now Ravenscourt Park), Turnham Green, Gunnersbury, Kew Gardens and Richmond. During the same year the Metropolitan was granted running powers over the same route, which it joined via a bridge to the west of Hammersmith (District) station, linked to a station at Hammersmith (Grove Road) and beyond to Shepherd's Bush and the City Line. Hammersmith (Grove Road) was owned by the London & South Western, as was the connecting bridge. Both have long been closed, but the remnants of the bridge can still be seen from the approach to Hammersmith on the District line eastbound, over which it once crossed heading northwards. Both the westbound District tracks and those added later for the Piccadilly run south of the bridge.

Beyond Turnham Green the District pressed onwards with new suburban stations at Acton Green (now Chiswick Park), Mill Hill Park (now Acton Town), Ealing Common and Ealing Broadway, which was reached in 1879.

The Hammersmith to Turnham Green line was all built over street level, and the station buildings were placed alongside the bridges carrying the tracks. A large brick booking hall still exists at Ravenscourt Park. Turnham Green has a small plastered white entrance to the old booking hall; each has platforms with serrated valanced canopies. These stations were built between 1869 and 1873. Kew Gardens has a medium-sized two-storey brick building erected in 1868 by the London & South Western. A similar building existed at Gunnersbury, its two island platforms being covered by curved canopies. In the mid-1960s the old buildings were demolished in connection with a redevelopment scheme.

In 1875 the first Earl's Court station was burnt down. Temporary repairs were made until a new station west of Earl's Court Road could be opened in 1878. The following year the Metropolitan opened the stations now served by the Jubilee Line at Willesden Green, Kilburn (& Brondesbury) and West Hampstead, as well as Finchley Road. The line moved further out in 1880 with stations at Kingsbury & Neasden (now Neasden) and Harrow (Harrow-on-the-Hill). In that year the District opened new stations at Walham Green (now Fulham Broadway), Parsons Green and Putney Bridge & Fulham. The latter is shown as it looked soon after the suffix was changed to '& Hurlingham' in 1902 (the station is now plain 'Putney Bridge'). There was no real need for a 'house style' when this station was built, and it features a large, but quite plain brick façade. Decoration is in the form of large signboards, and the building stands below platform level on the west side of the tracks.

As already mentioned, all this activity detracted attention from the need to complete the Inner Circle. The feud between the Metropolitan and the District hinged on two personalities, the chairmen of the companies. In 1871 the District, advocating more control over its own affairs, forced the resignation from the board of the Metropolitan directors. The following year it appointed James Staats Forbes, general manager of the London, Chatham & Dover Railway, as chairman, and in a counter-move the Metropolitan appointed his arch-opponent, Sir Edward Watkin of the South Eastern Railway. Forbes has been described as the 'master of bunkum', as his light-hearted touches could make almost anything seem plausible, but Watkin was far more dour. Their personal animosity had already

Rickmansworth The late 1880s saw continued expansion by the Metropolitan, and this building, dating from 1887, is a typical example of the company's suburban stations

Chesham When this station was completed in 1889 it was the furthest outpost of the Metropolitan. It retained this position for three years only, until the next extension to the main line opened

shown itself in Kent, and their mutual dislike meant trouble for the Inner Circle project. With the 'Chatham' already linked to the District, Forbes immediately set about making the western extensions in order to reinforce the District's 'declaration of independence'. However, Watkin's plans were far more grandiose. As chairman also of the Manchester, Sheffield & Lincolnshire Railway (later to become the Great Central), he was gradually extending this line southwards and the Metropolitan northwards. The idea was to link these to the South Eastern, providing a through service from Manchester to Dover. Furthermore, he was a sponsor of a Channel Tunnel project. If all these visions had materialized one would have been able to travel from Manchester to Calais without changing trains!

Watkin in particular did his best to prevent completion of the Inner Circle, but his hand was forced by an Act of 1879 which not only authorized the joint construction of the line from Aldgate to Mansion House but also obliged the companies to provide services over each other's sections. The Metropolitan still remained uncooperative and quickly built its own line to Tower Hill, with a temporary station called the Tower of London constructed in only three nights and two days and opened in September 1882. (The present Tower Hill station, opened in 1967, stands on this site.) It was only in use for two years until stations at Cannon Street, Eastcheap (now Monument) and Mark Lane (later Tower Hill) were opened in 1884, completing the Inner Circle.

Stations on what is now the East London section of the Metropolitan were served from the same month as the opening of the final link in the Inner Circle – October 1884. The stations were built by the East London Railway, though only Rotherhithe still has its original surface entrance in use. This is really no more than a shell, for the inside of this station has been rebuilt as part of a scheme to modernize the East London line. A sandy coloured brick was used for the exterior of the original buildings, but apart from modern panelling on the platforms the old brickwork is still very much in evidence. Another noteworthy feature is the massive iron buttresses which stretch between the retaining walls at intervals on the line (for example, at the northern end of Shadwell station).

At Wapping a plaque commemorates the building of the first tunnel under the Thames. This was devised by Sir Marc Brunel and engineered for a time by his son, Isambard Kingdom. A rectangular iron framework in which the miners worked as the tunnel pressed forward marked the first use of a tunnelling 'shield', which was later to form the basis of all 'tube' railways. The project was beset with problems, including a disastrous flood that killed seven men. By the time it was opened in 1843 funds had run out, and the only access that could be afforded were twin curved iron stairways leading down from street level. With no road

Wimbledon Park This station, built by the London & South Western Railway in 1889, was used by the District from the same year. The building at Southfields was identical

traffic to support it, the tunnel became known as 'Brunel's White Elephant'. Eventually the East London Railway took it over, running trains through it from Wapping to New Cross (London, Brighton & South Coast station, now New Cross Gate) via Rotherhithe and Surrey Docks. Wapping station retains both the old staircases and the original entrance to the tunnel, and these are now listed by the Department of the Environment as having historical interest.

Access to the East London line was via two new stations, at Aldgate East and St Mary's, linked to the Metropolitan from Liverpool Street and the District from Mark Lane. From St Mary's trains could either run straight on to the section or continue to Whitechapel. At Aldgate East a single-storey building was erected to include the booking office, with brickwork similar to that at Putney Bridge. The entrance was by a single opening in the middle of the building with an arched window above, and the balustrade along the top was of brick. The whole front was later to be rebuilt, and both this station and St Mary's were closed when a new Aldgate East opened between them in 1938.

Both the District and the Metropolitan provided a service over the line, the District terminating at New Cross (Gate), the Metropolitan running to another New Cross Station administered by Watkin's South Eastern Railway. The former has several platforms and an old brick station building and the latter is similar but with a timber-faced building to one side of it. By 1913

Wood Siding Sited next to the bridge over the GWR main line, this was probably the least substantial station ever served by the Metropolitan. This view shows its appearance in 1935 at about the time of its closure.
It consisted of a single platform, a hut and a level crossing

Ruislip Dating from 1904, this station is identical to the original terminal station at Uxbridge, which was closed in 1938

the Metropolitan was running the line alone, and the old Shoreditch station was added.

Platforms at stations near the river have open gutters running along them, as the ground is riddled with underground streams. A pump house exists at Rotherhithe station to clear the tunnel, and water running into that station is almost pure and drinkable, the London Transport chemist regularly checking the purity.

Despite this activity in East London the relentless drive outwards elsewhere continued. The District opened stations between 1883 and 1886 on a line to Hounslow Barracks with intermediate stations at Heston Hounslow (now Hounslow Central), Osterley & Spring Grove, Boston Road and South Ealing. There was also a branch from this to Hounslow (Town) station used only between 1883-6 and 1903-9. None of the stations on this line, which were all standard suburban brick buildings with pitched roofs similar to other District extension stations, survives in its original form. Their rebuilding took place later, mainly in the 1920s and 1930s.

For two years only, between 1883 and 1885, the District service was also extended over the Great Western tracks to Windsor. This involved using the Great Western station at Ealing Broadway next to the District's own (the former is illustrated on p. 51) and running via its other stations, mainly of standard pitched-roof brick-built Great Western type. These were: Castle Hill (Ealing Dean), Hanwell, Southall, Hayes & Harlington, two West Draytons (one replaced the other in 1884), Langley, and two Sloughs (in the same way as West Drayton). Castle Hill (Ealing Dean) was renamed West Ealing in 1899.

As Forbes' District moved on, Watkin was driving the Metropolitan further northwards as part of his grand design. By 1885 it had reached Pinner, two years later Northwood and Rickmansworth, and in 1889 Chorleywood and Chalfont Road (now '& Latimer') were completed. Rickmansworth is a well-preserved example of the standard stations of the line. All were built with a main entrance alongside the line, set into a long single-storey brick building from which the platform canopies projected. These were supported in turn by iron columns and brackets, and thus resembled other suburban stations of that era. At Harrow in 1880 the central entrance door had stood out from the whole building, with ornamentation above it and below the sloping eaves. These more recent stations, such as Rickmansworth, were smaller with booking hall entrances either in the centre or offset to one side. Over this was a small canopy, which in the case of Rickmansworth rested on an iron frame and pillars. Another common feature of all stations of this time is, of course, the presence of chimneys projecting up through the roof.

Past Chalfont Road a terminal station was opened on the same day as this and Chorleywood, 8 July 1889. This was Chesham, a small station with only one platform and

EARL'S COURT

Main entrance When reconstructed under Leslie Green the station entrance was given a brown facing with elaborate balustrading and 'Arts and Crafts' lettering. The arched windows were also a feature of Green's dark red tube station buildings

In its long history Earl's Court station has seen many changes. After the original wooden building burnt down in 1875 the station was resited, and much of it dates from 1878. One of the most impressive features to remain is the massive roof, which spans all four platforms between the retaining walls. The outside appearance was altered in readiness for the opening of the Great Northern, Piccadilly & Brompton Railway on 15 December 1906. This was a 'tube' railway, owned by the same concern as the District, and work was supervised by the chief architect, Leslie W. Green.

At the western end of the station a high-level walkway was constructed to serve the Earl's Court Exhibition Hall in Warwick Road, some distance from the old station. This resulted in alterations to the western end of the platforms and the construction of an entrance in Warwick Road, opened in 1937. Further major work was carried out

Warwick Road entrance This modest construction dates from the late 1930s, when the Underground had established itself as a leader of modern architecture in Britain. The booking office is reached along a walkway behind it, nearer the station proper

Lifts and ticket windows The present-day contribution to Earl's Court is a rebuilt ticket office in the main hall, associated with two new automatic lifts. The finishings are in brown and beige melamine

in 1982 in connection with the installation of new high-speed lifts for the Piccadilly Line.

On 4 October 1911 Earl's Court received the first public escalators, or 'moving stairs', on the Underground. They linked the District platforms to the Piccadilly, but the public was wary of them and a man with a wooden leg, who was known as 'Bumper' Harris, was employed to ride up and down all day demonstrating how safe it was. Some old ladies were not encouraged in the slightest, because they had a suspicion about how Mr Harris had lost his other leg!

Roof and platforms This view, looking back towards the main hall, displays many features. The platform indicators are of a type installed on electrification in the early 1900s, station names being shown on blue enamelled panels with white lettering, and are fitted to the subway frame which leads to the Piccadilly Line below

West Harrow The original halts on the Uxbridge line all had a similar appearance. Most were later rebuilt as full-sized stations, but West Harrow, opened in 1913, has changed little

a goods yard, intended to be served by a shuttle service to Chalfont Road. Outwardly it appears that Chesham has hardly ever seen alterations. The conversion of the goods yard into a car park just beyond the station proper is probably the only major change. Opposite the platform remains the signal box, and the canopy with its serrated valance is still in position to shelter waiting passengers. The entrance to the booking hall is a miniature version of the others back down the line, and as it is set next to, but almost perpendicular to, the platform the extended entrance canopy (continued here down from the roof) takes up almost the whole width of the building. The site of Chesham station is on the side of a hill above the town centre – an awkward position for building, and one which was only agreed to by the Metropolitan when the townspeople raised enough money to buy the land, bringing the station nearer than the company had originally planned.

Also in 1889, an extension to the London & South Western to a station at Wimbledon was opened. The District, under a joint agreement, extended its services over this line which involved four stations and a bridge over the Thames. Apart from Wimbledon itself there were intermediate stations at East Putney, Southfields and Wimbledon Park. These three remain as built, although the terminus was later to be reconstructed (see p. 72). At East Putney the booking hall was below platform level, whereas Southfields and Wimbledon Park had identical buildings on bridges above the line. These were small brick buildings with 'pyramid' roofs and tall chimney stacks. Each still carries its marking – 'LSWR 1889'. The island platforms and canopies are also original, and at the end of the platform at Wimbledon Park stands the signal box.

Meanwhile Watkin's great plans to link the Manchester, Sheffield & Lincolnshire to the Metropolitan continued. The Metropolitan opened new stations at Amersham, Great Missenden, Wendover, Stoke Mandeville and Aylesbury in 1892, with station types continuing from those of three years earlier. The following year the main line company secured its Act for more than ninety miles of new line to join the Metropolitan at Quainton Road, and in 1894 the Metropolitan changed to using the 1863 Great Western station at Aylesbury. It could then continue to a new station at Quainton Road on the site of an earlier one belonging to the Aylesbury & Buckingham railway. This company's former stations, built in 1868, were also used by the Metropolitan at Granborough Road and Winslow Road. Its station at Verney Junction, jointly built in the same year as the other two, became the terminus for the Metropolitan – a distance from Baker Street of over fifty miles. In 1897 an intermediate station – Waddesdon (Manor) – was built between Aylesbury and Quainton Road.

The Metropolitan took over the running of the former Wotton Tramway in 1899. Originally built in the 1870s by the Duke of

Ironwork over the entrance to South Kensington The design of this entrance showed an increasing awareness of the 'Arts and Crafts' movement in Britain, which became a feature common in Underground architecture in the early 1900s

Buckingham to serve his estate, there were plans to develop the line through to Oxford but it remained rural, with occasional sidings from the track to serve local farmers. There were stations, or halts, at Waddesdon (Road), Westcott, Wotton, Wood Siding and Brill, where the line ended. None consisted of more than a platform and minor building. Wood Siding is probably the most minimal station ever associated with the Underground. It was situated just at the bridge where the Brill Branch (as it became known) crossed the GWR main line to Banbury. Metropolitan stations never became more rural than in this peaceful neighbourhood.

After Watkin's retirement following a stroke in 1894 the Manchester company changed its name to the Great Central Railway and became unwilling to use Baker Street as its London terminus. Consequently, when it finally reached London (the last main line company to do so) in 1899, it was using its own station at Marylebone.

Since 1890 the first successful 'tube' railway, the City & South London, had been operating a fully electric system. This showed the shareholders of the Metropolitan and District the advantages of electric traction, particularly as the two sub-surface lines were beginning to run at a loss. At about this time very strong rumours were circulated about a takeover of the District by the Great Central, Great Western and South Eastern jointly.

Ealing Broadway This station building, the second on the site, is no longer in use as a booking hall. However, the District Line continues to serve the platforms behind it

Baron's Court Leslie Green, architect to the Underground Group, influenced the design of this station. It was built especially to serve both the District and the new Piccadilly railway

Forbes had no intention of being taken over by the main lines, and the most likely saviour was electrification. This had already been under consideration for some time, but the two companies were unable to agree whether to opt for overhead cables or a 'third rail' system. Now that Watkin was out of the way a peace formula was worked out involving the introduction of Continental 'Ganz' overhead cables.

With one obstacle overcome, another problem remained. Funds were running short, and the opening of the Central London Railway (another electric Tube) in 1900 attracted away much of the District's revenue. Forbes turned to America for help from a consortium led by Charles Tyson Yerkes, and by the beginning of 1901 the company was financially more stable. Forbes' position was not so sound. In an apparent coup Yerkes ousted him from the chairmanship in March 1901 and the electrification plans were thrown into chaos. The new chairman was a hard-hitting financier who brought with him a reputation for using the most devious methods in handling his affairs. It would appear that the very name 'Yerkes' was enough to strike terror into those concerned with British railways. Forbes had always seemed rather a scoundrel, but at least he was a 'railwayman'. Public relations with the District deteriorated rapidly as Yerkes lost no time in winning a case for an American system of electrification involving four rails. On 15 July 1901 he created the Metropolitan District Electric Traction Company to carry out the necessary conversion work, and then went on to secure shares in the new tube lines as well. The Metropolitan rejected his takeover bid, remaining fiercely independent.

An extension of the District from Ealing Common to South Harrow, involving standard suburban stations at North Ealing (the only original station building here remaining today), Park Royal & Twyford Abbey, Perivale-Alperton, Sudbury Town and Sudbury Hill, had been almost ready for opening in 1899. This was delayed, and electric tracks were installed for trials and the training of motormen. The line opened for passenger traffic in 1903.

Slightly further north the Metropolitan opened a line from Harrow-on-the-Hill to Uxbridge in 1904 with another full-sized station in between at Ruislip. The age of 'Metro-land' was under way, the railway's publicity describing the town as 'Ruislip – London's Healthiest Suburb'. The brick station is one of the best preserved of the original Metropolitan suburban stations.

The concept of 'Metro-land' was a result of the company's policy of attracting people to areas where there had been only countryside and small villages before. Its success is blurred by the problem of cause and effect. Did the railway encourage the growth of the suburbs or vice versa? A series of halts were built along the Uxbridge branch: Ickenham (1905), Eastcote and Rayners Lane (1906), Ruislip Manor (1912) and West Harrow (1913). They were all of similar construction, a pebble-dashed booking hut with tiled roof, and situated either above or down at the side of the tracks. West Harrow is the only one to remain as built; like the others, it was erected before all the houses, shops and other buildings now surrounding them were there. Hillingdon station was added in 1923.

Intermediate stations were opened at Preston Road in 1908 and Dollis Hill in 1909, and others, reflecting an adaptation of architectural developments on the line in town, followed at North Harrow in 1915 and Northwick Park in 1923. A halt set up to serve a golf club, Sandy Lodge, was constructed in 1910. It became known later as Moor Park and was not rebuilt until 1961.

Electrification and the end of steam brought an opportunity to give the system a facelift. From just before the turn of the century the District stations began to undergo alterations. Among the first were Gloucester Road and South Kensington. The ironwork above the new entrances to South Kensington concealed the arched glass roof over the shopping arcade that ran between them. The booking hall was set below and to the side of this, with a further entrance from the long subway to the museums, which 'every schoolboy knows' opened in 1885. Another fine arcade was built at High Street Kensington, where by arrangement with the Metropolitan the station was enlarged and entirely reconstructed. Work continued through 1904, and the laurel motifs outside the station within the arcade read 'MR' and 'DR' and are dated 1906, when work was completed. The frontage of red brick and Portland stone fitted in well with surrounding Kensington.

The external appearance of several older District Railway stations altered radically during this period. At Fulham Broadway an imposing symmetrical façade was built, faced in brown tiles. The booking hall was constructed like an arcade with a glass roof, along the side of which was a row of ticket

Temple Custom designed to blend with Somerset House, this station is one of several that were rebuilt along the Embankment

Whitechapel Reconstructed in 1902, this station was to serve the Metropolitan (East London), District and Whitechapel & Bow lines

windows set in a dark wooden frame with ornamental 'DR' motifs above them. The roof and platforms were left as constructed in 1879. This roof was a smaller version of its massive contemporary at Earl's Court, an angled iron and glass construction (see p. 21) which was also reduced in scale to cover the terminal platforms at Ealing Broadway. Here the District station is almost as built inside. Outside, however, the original 1879 building was demolished and rebuilt on the same site. This first building had consisted of two two-storey buildings with 'pyramid' roofs, linked by a brick façade with two arches jutting out parallel from it to form the entrance. Both the upper and lower floor windows (the latter arched) were almost obscured by large signs advertising train fares and services, and a shop had been built into part of the building when it was decided to reconstruct it. The external design of the second building, particularly the flat-topped parapet, was similar to Fulham Broadway, but at Ealing the façade was built of white stone with the station name built into the top of it. The entrance was in the centre, flanked by provision for shops (a feature common to many rebuilt stations). The building still stands today, though access to the District line has been from the station rebuilt alongside it, on the site of the old GWR station, since that was opened in 1966.

The 'Arts and Crafts' lettering used at South Kensington was liberally applied to the new Tube stations built by Yerkes' companies. It was also applied to the brown frontage at a rebuilt Aldgate East, as well as three stations through which the Great Northern, Piccadilly & Brompton Railway was to pass. At Hammersmith the entrances from the Broadway were reconstructed, and Earl's Court received a new frontage as well. In October 1905 the District opened a brand new station at Baron's Court to provide an interchange with the GNP & B (later to become the Piccadilly Line) when it began operations the following year. Its appearance is of a smaller version of Earl's Court (shown on p. 20), complete with balustrading but with shallower windows above the shops.

The District's stations were rebuilt with varying designs to suit their site and surroundings, as was the intention of Harry W. Ford, the District's architect. The main entrance to Westminster (formerly Westminster Bridge) station was doubled in width in 1909 to form a proper booking hall, rather than the passage that had been there before.

The station at Temple was entirely reconstructed between 1911 and 1912 to provide a much enlarged and improved booking hall at its eastern end. Two shops were built into it here, and the rest of the building stretched away covering the length of the station. It was finished in white stone with a series of arched windows along its south side, facing the river. The parapet of this long single-storey building consists of balustrading which acts as a guard rail when one walks on to the flat roof. The northern edge of the station is only just above street level, with access from a few steps. It is possible to see the trains pulling into the station below through the two vents which come up through this roof. The style of the building here was chosen to complement the design of nearby Somerset House.

The original entrance and exit to Monument station took the form of two brick arches, only one of which remains, in 'Monument Station Buildings'. Modernization here included a new façade of Portland stone, much in keeping with the nearby financial institutions. The building still

Bow Road Built by the Whitechapel & Bow in 1902, this station is served by the District. It is a sister station of Stepney Green, but only the Bow Road building is listed by the DoE

remains (the word 'station' still ghosted on the white stonework) but since 1935 a new underground booking hall has been in use, with access provided by new subway entrances opened at the same time.

The decision to extend the District service eastwards was taken before electrification began at Whitechapel. In 1902 a new combined station entrance was opened to serve the combined Metropolitan (East London), District and Whitechapel & Bow railways. Behind the standard white brick front were a series of passages and staircases connecting the east–west platforms to those of the East London section, which run immediately below and perpendicular to them.

The plan was to run the District through three new Whitechapel & Bow Railway stations (Stepney Green, Mile End and Bow Road) and thence through existing London, Tilbury & Southend Railway stations to Upminster. This meant that none of the stations was actually built by the District.

Of the three new 1902 stations, Mile End has since been rebuilt (in 1946 in connection with extensions to the Central Line), but both Stepney Green and Bow Road survive in their original form. They have similar buildings; Bow Road is now the subject of a Department of the Environment preservation order. The exterior of Bow Road is of red brick with a stone eaves cornice and a hipped slate roof. The two round-arched doors have terracotta architraves and keystones with decorative fanlights. Windows are set into two arches. Inside, an enclosed wooden bridge crosses the platforms, which themselves are covered partly by a barrel-vaulted brick roof and partly by serrated valanced wooden canopies. Support for the canopies is by hexagonal columns with panelled plinths and capitals; there are fourteen of them on one platform but only twelve on the other because of the curvature of the track through the station.

The London, Tilbury & Southend stations which were used by the District were much older. From Bow Road the District ran through Bromley (later 'by-Bow'), West Ham, Plaistow, Upton Park, East Ham, Barking, Dagenham (now East) and Hornchurch to Upminster. Platform canopy support brackets featured either cog and wheel or LTSR motifs. Upton Park, built in 1877, is a nicely ornamented brick station with brown and cream tiling in the old large booking hall. The original wooden canopies hang over the platforms, packed most Saturdays with supporters travelling to and from the nearby matches at West Ham Football Club. Two extra platforms were added in 1903.

The main District service from Barking to Upminster was withdrawn on electrification in 1905, but occasional District trains were worked past this line as far as Southend from 1910 and Shoeburyness from 1911 as a through service. All intermediate stations were served at some time, but the provision was withdrawn in 1939. Meanwhile, the other end of the District was extended. Provisions for a new Harrow & Uxbridge Railway authorized by an Act of 1897 never materialized. This scheme was part of a larger one intended to build a line from South Harrow through Uxbridge, Denham, Gerrards Cross, Beaconsfield

Upton Park Built in 1877 by the London, Tilbury & Southend Railway, this station has been used by the District since 1902

Hounslow Central One of a new generation of District Railway stations, this reconstruction of 1912 is today served by the Piccadilly Line

and Loudwater to High Wycombe. The idea was curtailed because of the opposition of the Great Western and in its place a length of railway line was constructed between South Harrow and Rayners Lane, enabling the District to run a through service to Uxbridge over the Metropolitan tracks, beginning on 3 March 1910.

1908 and 1909 saw the opening by the District of two new intermediate stations on the Hounslow line at Northfield (Ealing) and Hounslow Town (now Hounslow East), which replaced the old station of the same name in the High Street. The latter building survives but with a recently rebuilt entrance. Heston Hounslow (now Hounslow Central) was rebuilt in 1912, and reveals the altering trend in suburban station design. Its external appearance of a neo-Georgian cottage is similar to designs that were later to be built by both the Metropolitan and the tube companies, removing the hitherto rather weighty image of suburban stations. The same year saw the opening of a joint London & South Western/District station at Stamford Brook in association with the separation of the two companies' tracks.

There are two stretches of line brought into use in the early 1900s that are not part of the system today. The first was a short spur from Mill Hill Park (Acton Town) to a new station at South Acton, opened by the District in 1905, which survived until 1959. In 1906 a Metropolitan service from Latimer Road was provided to the West London Railway stations at Uxbridge Road and Kensington (Addison Road), now known as Kensington (Olympia) and later served by the District. The Metropolitan service was withdrawn in 1947.

The rejuvenation of many of the old District stations after electrification has already been dealt with. From about 1911 the Metropolitan began giving its older stations a new appearance. The crowning glory was Baker Street, the company's headquarters, which took seventeen years to complete (including the flats above). A standard external appearance was adopted by C.W. Clark, the company's architect, involving white facing and built-in lettering. Great Portland Street is his remodelling of the old Portland Road (the name changed in 1917). With entrances on each side, it is particularly striking as it occupies

BAKER STREET

Exterior The ground floor of the building originally included a parcel distribution office and a shopping arcade. The latter is now mainly occupied by the Bakerloo/Jubilee booking hall

Plaque of Remembrance As a reminder that the Metropolitan was an independent company the station gained several special features, such as this tribute to company employees killed in the First World War

The building we know as Baker Street station assumed its present form during extensive reconstruction work undertaken after 1911. Responsibility fell to the Metropolitan's own architect, C.W. Clark, who produced what John Betjeman regarded as a product of the Edwardian age.

The brochure published for the official stone-laying ceremony in 1912 described the proposed building as 'carried out in Portland stone in a free treatment of Italian Renaissance, with arches . . . heavily rusticated, and columns continuing through four storeys'. The main elevation of the Company's offices would be 'Neo-Grec', and over the original porch (now demolished) a space was reserved for the company's new electric traction-orientated armorial bearings. Curiously, the old device has shown two steam trains in separate tunnels, which the original Metropolitan did not have. The *Railway* Gazette described as 'most striking' the use of railway symbols such as buffers and coupling hook which decorated the building.

Initially, plans involved a hotel on the upper floors, but work stopped in 1914 on the outbreak of war. It was late in the 1920s before Chiltern Court – a block of flats – was completed in its stead. Among the first residents was the author H.G. Wells.

Baker Street was the headquarters of the Metopolitan Railway, a company that still had main line aspirations, but the tube railways were already encroaching on its territory. Through bookings were allowed with the Bakerloo when it opened in 1906, originally at its own adjacent station. Subsequently, however, it was to be absorbed into the main complex.

Metropolitan/Circle platforms This is the oldest surviving part of the station. Daylight originally streamed down through the shafts at either side, and the effect is being recreated artificially during a restoration programme that began on 10 January 1983, exactly 120 years after the line first opened.

Main booking hall The booking hall was provided with shops, a bar, and a tea room – the Metropolitan's trains ran for over fifty miles from Baker Street, and customers would expect main line service before such a journey

Metropolitan suburban platforms The Metropolitan's St John's Wood Railway opened in 1868, and these open platforms could be used either as a terminus or as a link to the Inner Circle. The pillars were added when the station was rebuilt

Great Portland Street C.W. Clark's rebuilt Portland Road was part of a massive reconstruction programme by the Metropolitan that took place in the years around the First World War

an 'island' site. Other stations had fairly flat façades, as at Paddington (Praed Street), Edgware Road and Farringdon Street. The latter was given a facelift in 1922 transforming it into Farringdon & High Holborn, a name it still bears today, though the suffix has been dropped. This is probably the most typical of the new Metropolitan exteriors, one of which was provided at Willesden Green. Here the station proudly displays the slogan 'Metropolitan Railway', despite the fact that from 1939 it was served only by the Bakerloo Line, and from 1979 the Jubilee Line. Wherever one finds stations with features reminiscent of these stations one can be sure they are the work of C.W. Clark.

The inside of Farringdon was also refurbished. All Metropolitan stations were redecorated with new wooden ticket windows and small vertical green 'mosaic' tiles, including Bayswater (which was never substantially altered on the outside).

Further developments now slowed down, as the Metropolitan and District had reached what were to prove their outer limits. Both companies had largely rebuilt their original stations as well, and so it is appropriate to leave them and to focus attention instead on to the early stations of the tube railways.

Farringdon Rebuilt by Clark as Farringdon & High Holborn in 1922, this façade is typical of several other Metropolitan stations of the period

2 The Advent of the Tubes

The two railways discussed so far – the Metropolitan and the District – differ substantially from the remainder of London's Underground. They are both known as 'sub-surface' railways, for their tunnels run just below the surface. In town their stations need nothing more than a flight of steps for the traveller to descend to platform level. Rolling stock – 'surface stock' – is built to larger dimensions than on other Underground lines in accordance with the tunnel size. For most of its length the Inner Circle has trains running side by side in both directions in the covered excavations known as 'cut and cover' workings.

The Northern, Central, Bakerloo, Piccadilly, Victoria and Jubilee lines all run below central London in deep 'tube' tunnels with circular, rather than rectangular, cross-sections. The use of two adjacent tunnels serving trains travelling in opposite directions is standard practice for most of the network, and these restrictions led to a different station layout from that of the two older lines. From entry at the surface a passenger would have to descend to deep level by lift (or later, escalator) and walk along subways cut into the ground which connected the platforms. These were formed by enlarging the tube diameter at stations, so the whole excavation below ground became a 'warren'. The first four lines mentioned assumed much of their present form when constructed and opened between 1890 and 1907 – a remarkably short space of time considering that the most recent tube built (the Jubilee Line from Baker Street to Charing Cross) took seven years to complete with modern equipment. This flurry of activity around the turn of the century resulted not only in the first steps towards a united system but also in the first planned attempts at a corporate and identifiable 'Underground' image.

The opening of six stations – Stockwell, (Kennington) Oval, Kennington (New Street), Elephant & Castle, Borough and King William Street – heralded the arrival of the tube age. These stations were owned by the City & South London Railway, opened in December 1890, which was the world's first successful tube railway and the first to use electric motive power.

The honour of the world's very first tube railway went to an abortive attempt at a steam-worked service under the Thames near the Tower. This opened in 1870 and was engineered by Peter William Barlow, who had modified Brunel's idea of a 'tunnelling shield'. Barlow's tunnel was circular, rather than rectangular, in section and was lined with cast-iron segments whereas Brunel's had had bricks. Passengers

Oval When built all CSLR stations had a common appearance. The exterior at Oval was radically altered at a later date

Kennington A listed building, this is the only CSLR station to retain so much of its character. It is also the only one still to have its distinctive dome

descended by a lift and were transported under the river in a cable-hauled car. The scheme was soon abandoned because of technical difficulties, and although the tunnel continued to be used by pedestrians until 1894, it now carries hydraulic and water mains.

A pupil of Barlow's, James Henry Greathead, continued the shield idea and gave his name to it. Greathead shields were to be used in the construction of all the successful Tube railways. When the City of London & Southwark Subway Company was incorporated in July 1884, it appointed Greathead as engineer. To avoid legal arguments it was decided to run the new railway as near as possible under existing streets, although at one point the tunnels carrying traffic in opposite directions had to be built on top of one another in order to keep within the narrow road width. As it was not to be connected with any other railways, a narrow gauge and tunnel size were selected, causing problems later when the railway became part of the Northern Line and the tunnels had to be enlarged to what was to become standard *tube* size. Rolling stock was ordered with heavily upholstered interiors and very small ventilators, on the assumption that there would be nothing to see inside the tunnels. The cars were consequently nicknamed 'padded cells'.

The City & South London Railway, as it had become, was opened by the Prince of Wales on 4 November 1890, though passenger services did not begin for over a month. This royal patronage was a great boost for the company, and crowds of people were soon travelling on what became called the 'sardine-box railway'.

The stations on the Surrey side were rather grand and attractive. The architect appointed to the company was T. Phillips Figgis, who designed similar surface buildings on corner sites for each station. The red-brick, one-storey building with white stone dressings at Kennington typified them. The entrance from the corner is canted, and is the most altered feature of the exterior, having been altered in the 1920s with a new canopy and tiling when the line was modernized. Along Braganza Street are five bays, defined by pilasters resting on plinths with supporting entablature and a brick parapet. Further along from these is another set back entrance bay with a round-arched, rusticated doorway. Under the single elliptical arch in Kennington Park Road is a shop. The lift mechanism for the station is housed in a large lead dome resting on a roughcast drum and surmounted by a small cupola.

The building at Kennington is now listed by the Department of the

Environment, as it is the only one of the original City & South London stations to retain so much of its character. The station did not entirely escape later modernization, with both the entrance already mentioned and the booking hall being altered slightly. Also, two double doors were inserted into the dome to give access to the lift machinery, and the lifts themselves were replaced in 1982-3. Of the other original surface buildings of the line on this side of the river, both Stockwell and Elephant & Castle have been replaced, and the appearances of Borough and Oval were substantially altered in the 1920s. However, part of the exterior wall at Oval along Harleyford Street remains, and inside the back wall of the booking hall curves around where the lift shaft once was. This has since been replaced by escalators. None of the stations besides Kennington retains its dome – their most conspicuous feature when they were built.

Below ground the subsequent enlargement of the old tunnels has removed the original platform level features. Although separate platform tunnels were provided at intermediate stations, Stockwell had a narrow wooden 'island' platform between the tracks, and 'island' platforms of this kind, with no division, are still found on the Northern Line today. Above this was a row of suspended gas lamps with 'crown'-like decorations around them. The use of gas lamps in an electric railway station may seem surprising, but is explained by the fact that the company's generating plant at Stockwell was working at full stretch just to supply enough current for the trains, let alone anything else. Platform tunnels had square white tiles to maximise available light, with a single strip of decorated brown tiles half way down. Lifts were originally hydraulically operated, and by all accounts were pleasantly decorated with wooden panelling.

The station at King William Street, north of the river, proved very awkward to use. Not only did its single platform slow down return journeys from the terminus, but the tunnel gradient rising from under the river proved too much of a strain for the electric locomotives, which constantly gave trouble here. Accordingly, when a northward extension was planned it was decided to abandon this station completely, and the railway was rerouted north of Borough to London Bridge, Bank and Moorgate, three stations opened in February 1900. Both London Bridge and Bank, unlike their predecessors, had both platforms adjacent on the same level, in the manner adopted by all the later tube railways. The station at Bank still exists, attached by a subway to the main booking hall. The entrances

Pillar capital at Bank This is inside the original CSLR booking hall at Bank, which is situated underground below the Church of St Mary Woolnoth

Moorgate This building was the headquarters of the CSLR, and despite extensive booking hall alterations still looks much as it was when built in 1900. The architect was T. Phillips Figgis, who had also designed other stations for the company

were small classical structures, built to blend in with Wren's church of St Mary Woolnoth on the corner of Lombard Street and King William Street. One was built on either side of the main entrance of the church, with a main entrance in King William Street leading to an underground booking hall with the roof supported by heavy iron columns. The original lift shafts continue in use today, and the booking hall gives an adequate feeling of these stations as built.

The grandest building was at Moorgate, where the company headquarters were set up. It still contains entrances to the later integrated Moorgate station and forms a centrepiece between the subway entrance on the eastern side of Moorgate and the modern Metropolitan entrance. Figgis designed a six-storey, red-brick building with Portland stone dressings. The ground floor was stone-faced with arched entrances (now blocked off), and above it continuous cill bands ran under the windows, each with architraves and cornices, and the top storey was built gable-ended, with a slate roof. On the corner of Moorgate itself was a round corner tower standing proud from the rest of the building and supported by attached columns below, flanking what is now a shop entrance. This carefully considered building has joined Figgis' Kennington Station on the Department of the Environment list.

In June 1900 the two new stations at Clapham Road (now North) and Clapham Common were opened south of Stockwell, and in November 1901 the northern end of the line was extended to the Angel, with intermediate stations at Old Street and City Road (now closed). The red-brick pattern of Figgis' earlier stations was continued here. The station at Old Street was built to provide interchange with another tube line then under construction. This was a deep-level tube large enough to take main line trains from Finsbury Park to Old Street via Drayton Park, Highbury (& Islington) and Essex Road. The Great Northern & City had obtained powers in 1892 and was opened in 1904, also running on to Moorgate.

In May 1907 the City & South London reached its limit as an independent company when its extension to King's Cross for St Pancras and Euston was opened. An increase in power capacity for the company meant that electric lights and Otis electric lifts could be installed at all the later stations. It was necessary to provide interchange facilities at both stations with the new Yerkes tube lines, which opened at about the same time. The Piccadilly railway had a station building on the forecourt of the Great Northern King's Cross, whereas the City & South London had an underground booking hall beneath the road between the two main line stations. It was reached by subway entrances from the two stations and the 'Piccadilly' tube, as well as open ones on the pavement. Single island platforms had been built at Clapham Common and Angel, and this procedure was fol-

Euston Sidney Smith's Euston building, opened in 1907, has since disappeared. At the time it differed markedly from other CSLR stations, with an affinity to Leslie Green's stations on other Underground lines

lowed at Euston. The surface building here has since disappeared. It was designed by Sidney Smith and was quite a departure from the company's previous stations, being faced all in white with a similar feeling to the stations on the Yerkes tubes. Here we are leaping ahead somewhat, for before we look at these we must consider the second major tube railway.

In 1898 a $1\frac{1}{2}$-mile line was opened between Waterloo and City stations (the latter now called Bank). This Waterloo & City line, popularly called 'the Drain', was promoted by the London & South Western Railway and had no physical connection with any other railway. Indeed, it has never formed part of the Underground, and for the purposes of this study needs only a passing mention as it was the second practical tube railway in London. However, two years later a long-desired railway under Oxford Street was opened. This was the Central London Railway.

Since 1865 rival promoters had been advocating schemes for a railway along this route, one of the most congested in London. After the initial success of the City & South London, the Central London at last received its Act to build a line from Shepherd's Bush Green to Cornhill, later gaining authority to extend to the Bank and beyond. Like the City & South London, the Central London invited the Prince of Wales to open the new railway, which he did on 27 June 1900.

The original stations of this new line were at Shepherd's Bush, Holland Park, Notting Hill Gate (where the tunnels were at their deepest, running above one another), Queen's Road (now Queensway), Lancaster Gate, Marble Arch, Bond Street, Oxford Circus, Tottenham Court Road, British Museum (now closed), Chancery Lane, Post Office (now St Paul's), and Bank. They were all of a basic standardized design conceived by Harry B. Measures. Originally the exteriors were all faced with large brown 'biscuit' stone, described by the company as 'a kind of Renaissance carried out in terracotta'. Indeed, this predominance of brown with the red brick of Delissa Joseph's additional floors, which were added at some stations, was in marked contrast to the white stone used as ornament at many contemporary stations. Above the entrances were a multitude of little stone carvings, including faces and cherubs, for although the ground plans of individual stations were small, this was no reason to cut back on decoration. Wood and tiling were in evidence throughout the booking halls, and large electric lifts were installed to transport passengers down to platform level. It was here that the difference between this railway and the City & South London was most marked, for the Central London had built its tunnels a little wider than the previous company. The small amount of extra space created on the trains was a big attraction, and lighting on trains and at stations was by electricity from the start, a pattern followed by all later tube lines. The 'Twopenny Tube' (it had

FEATURES OF CENTRAL LONDON RAILWAY STATIONS

Platform, St Paul's This demonstrates the all-over white tiling used for Central London platform tunnels, which can also still be seen at several other stations. St Paul's station itself was opened in 1900 as Post Office, and was not renamed until 1937

Exterior lamp bracket Lighting outside the stations took the form of arc lamps attached to brackets such as this. Also still found elsewhere, this particular example adorns the old building that was once the company's British Museum station. The name was presumably devised to drum up tourist trade for the museum

The surviving features of the original Central London Railway stations are often overshadowed by the better known, dark red glazed buildings of the tube lines that followed. The Central London did, however, have a distinctive style. As with many later examples, its station buildings were single-storey booking halls, but upper storeys were commissioned for most in order to match the exterior treatments.

The ornamentation outside the stations was perhaps rather fussy for a modern electric railway, but the buildings were designed both to present a common identity and to blend in with contemporary London. There was none of the more adventurous 'Arts and Crafts' style used by the later tubes, but the Central London was to prove itself a welcome and efficient railway distinctive enough to do without some of the more modern elements of design.

The interior décor of the stations was on the whole unadventurous, but the extensive use of tiling and wooden panelling was a feature common to all the early tubes. Lifts were provided at each station, and replacement with escalators has not affected all of them though more modern lifts have been installed in the old shafts. The complete tiling of platform tunnels in white followed the example of the City & South London tubes, but that company had been able to provide only gas lighting. The Central London was, from the start, an all-electric tube.

Decoration at Queensway Detailed and elaborate stonework can be found outside the original CLR stations; carved faces, each of them different, are dotted along the street façades

Lift door, Holland Park The Central London Railway kept several design features simple, such as this wooden-panelled lift door on the exit side at Holland Park

Booking hall, Queensway The curved ticket office at Queensway is not typical of CLR booking halls, but the brown/cream colour scheme and wooden-framed ticket windows are

Bond Street This demonstrates Measures' original station exteriors as they were opened in 1900. This façade was rebuilt about thirty years later, and again for the opening of the Jubilee Line in 1979

a universal flat fare of 2d.) was not just functional below ground, but seemed lighter and airier than its predecessor. Platforms were set on a 'hump' in the tunnel, which aided deceleration and acceleration of trains entering and leaving the station. The platform tunnels and subways themselves were all lined with rectangular white tiles in a 'brickwork' pattern, like the City & South London, but the brilliant electric lighting from suspended lamps made the surroundings far more bearable. The station names were shown on large enamelled signboards.

Incidentally, these new stations were the first to have the standard canopy over each entrance. Many stations have since had flat-sided, flat-topped canopies grafted on to them bearing the names of the station and line. The frameworks of these canopies contain revised translucent signboards at the old Central London stations, the original boards having shown the station names, the 'CLR' logo, and the word 'TUBE' picked out in white on a red panel.

Some platforms from these old stations survive with their basic white tiling, as at Bank, St Paul's, Chancery Lane and Lancaster Gate. At others the platform 'wall' has been redecorated, leaving the old tiles in place on the 'ceiling'. Several surface buildings from the railway are still in use. The one at Shepherd's Bush is painted cream, but early in 1983 the original facing at Holland Park was restored. This and Queensway are probably the nearest to complete Central London Railway stations still in existence. All other stations to Bond Street have been rebuilt, but Oxford Circus and Tottenham Court Road have their complete surface buildings (Oxford Circus is shown on page 110).

The old station building at British Museum at the junction of New Oxford Street and Holborn still stands; it is now in use as two

Holland Park No additional floors were ever added to this station. The exterior was for many years painted over in grey, but early in 1983 the paint was removed to show the original colouring

shops and a café. It was closed in 1933, when new platforms were opened to link the line to the Piccadilly at Holborn, but the old white tiled platforms can still be seen between Tottenham Court Road and Holborn on the Central Line.

The underground booking hall at Bank has been largely rebuilt since it was bombed during the Second World War, but its situation remains the same, below the open area in front of the Royal Exchange and the Bank of England. Bank station today is therefore made up of three sub-surface booking halls – those of the Waterloo & City, City & South London, and Central London Railways, as well as an escalator link to the District at Monument dating from 1933.

The Central London had problems in operation to start with. The rails were laid on longitudinal sleepers on a solid base. When combined with the weight of the electric locomotives, this caused unpleasant vibrations in surface buildings along its route. After being deluged with complaints the new locomotives were removed and 'multiple unit' trains were run instead. Current was supplied by a third rail, returning along the running rails, and substations were installed at various points along the line.

Once established the Central London began to consider expansion, but it was only to reach two stations as an independent company. Liverpool Street (to the east) was opened in 1912, and Wood Lane (at the western end) four years earlier. This station was built on a loop of track between the two platforms at Shepherd's Bush and the depot, and consequently had only one platform, traffic running from Shepherd's Bush through Wood Lane and straight on to Shepherd's Bush again. It was opened to serve the Franco-British Exhibition at White City in 1908, and was to remain in use for almost forty years. The station building is still there, and the old platform is still just visible as trains rush through a short tunnel between White City and the main tube at Shepherd's Bush. In 1928 the famous wooden platform extension was installed. The opening of White City Stadium had congested the station and more platform space was needed. This would not ordinarily have been possible, as the tight configuration of the loop for trains running to the depot restricted any normal extension. To overcome the problem a movable extension was built, which could be swung clear of the line whenever the points were set for a train to run through to the depot.

There were many other tube railway schemes promoted in the

Tottenham Court Road The old CLR entrance was converted to a subway entrance in the 1920s when the CLR and Hampstead Line combined booking hall was refurbished

Wood Lane The exterior of the station was rebuilt at the time of the First World War when the CLR became part of the Underground Group. The 'UndergrounD' roundels consist of mosaic, and although the station closed in 1947 this exterior is still in place

1890s, but only a few were successful in obtaining their Acts. Apart from the projects already mentioned, powers were granted to the following organizations: the Charing Cross, Euston & Hampstead, and the Baker Street & Waterloo (1893), the Brompton & Piccadilly Circus (1897), and the Great Northern & Strand (1899). These were to form the basis for the Northern, Bakerloo and Piccadilly Lines known today. Each railway would probably have developed independently, as the City & South London, Waterloo & City, Central London and Great Northern & City did, had it not been for the seemingly all-powerful influence of Charles Tyson Yerkes.

Yerkes was not content with owning merely the District Railway (which he had taken over in 1901), and determined to extend his interests to embrace as many tube railways as possible. In accordance, purchases were made of the powers for the Brompton & Piccadilly Circus, Great Northern & Strand, and the proposed Hampstead tube in September 1901, followed by the partly constructed Baker Street & Waterloo in March of the following year. On 9 April all these railways became part of his Underground Electric Railways Company of London Limited, with financial backing coming from Yerkes himself along with Speyer Bros of London, Speyer & Co. of New York, the Old Colony Trust Company of Boston, and later Teixeira de Mattos Bros of Amsterdam. Staving off much possible competition (for example, in early 1902 there were 26 Bills for 86 miles of tube railway under London, the main one – sponsored by London United Tramways – being blocked only by the purchase of that group by Speyer Bros), the Underground Group set about a policy of rationalization in working and design. After much negotiation with the Great Northern Railway, the Great Northern & Strand and Brompton & Piccadilly Circus schemes were merged in August 1902, with the name becoming Great Northern, Piccadilly & Brompton Railway in November. This move had two main effects. First, it resulted in the intended terminal of the former – Strand (now Aldwych) – being left on a short branch off the main route, forever to be served by a shuttle from Holborn. More important, the terms of the agreement forbade any extension north of Finsbury Park, as the Great Northern wanted no competition here. It was not until the 1930s that the Piccadilly was able to extend to Cockfosters.

Yerkes died at the end of December, and so did not live to see his tube railways opened. His place was taken by Edgar Speyer, ably assisted by Sir George Gibb (formerly general manager of the North Eastern Railway), and together they continued the work, with Gibb as general manager. Public relations with the Group (Yerkes had never been popular) accordingly became more cordial.

The first tube to be opened was the Baker Street & Waterloo on 10 March 1906, with engineering supervised by Harley H.

Dalrymple-Hay and stations designed by Leslie Green. Green had been educated at Dover College, and had served in his father's office for two years and studied for a year in Paris before starting his own practice in 1897. He had been appointed architect to the Group in 1903, and was to design over fifty stations for it. The first to be completed were these on the Baker Street & Waterloo.

The stations opened on that day were: Baker Street, Regent's Park, Oxford Circus, Piccadilly Circus, Trafalgar Square (now part of Charing Cross), Embankment, Waterloo, and Kennington Road (now Lambeth North). In August the line reached Elephant & Castle, at a station opposite that of City & South London, and in 1907 stations were opened at Great Central (now Marylebone) and Edgware Road. All the stations were built to the same standardized format, as were those of the other lines, which opened soon afterwards. Each new railway was announced with reprinted articles from railway publications, bearing the notice 'With the compliments of the Underground Electric Railways Company of London Ltd'. These bear witness to the attempts to achieve a corporate image for the three lines, for the description of each of the stations is virtually identical. I therefore make no apology for quoting this passage from the 'Baker Street & Waterloo Railway' in full:

> The passenger station buildings, and the interior walls of the stations themselves, have been designed by Mr Leslie W. Green, ARIBA, and they present a very handsome appearance. The ground plans of the buildings vary in shape and size according to the site available, but the elevations of those above ground are similar. Each station consists of a spacious ground floor, with a mezzanine floor above, the entrances, exits and windows being schemed to form a series of spacious arches. The roofs are left flat, so that additional storeys for occupation as offices or dwellings can be erected when desired. The structure consists of a steel framework which is clothed with terracotta glazed blocks of a dark but brilliant ruby-red colour. The large gilded letters forming the name of the station are in one piece with the blocks, and stand out in bold relief. These names, which are illuminated at night by arc lamps, run along above the entrances. The entrances and exits are very wide, and the booking halls are also spacious. Some of the stations have two lift shafts, with two lifts in each, while others have only one such shaft, but with three lifts in it. The diameter of the former shaft is 23 feet and of the latter 30 feet. All the station buildings are fireproof, the only wood in them being the joinery of doors and windows, and of the lift enclosures, which is of teak, uninflammable.

The same article goes on to describe the interior thus:

> The platforms are about 400 feet long and are of concrete . . . The walls are lined with cream-coloured enamelled

Piccadilly Circus This is one of three entrances to the original booking hall. It faced directly on to the Circus itself, and is still used as a subway entrance to the later sub-surface booking hall

COVENT GARDEN

Exterior At ground level the station has shops built into it, and a greengrocer's takes up the corner. The first floor is of arched windows and glazed bricks, and the structure has been further built upon

This is a well-preserved example of the type of station designed for the Underground Group by Leslie W. Green in the early 1900s. It was not quite finished for the opening of the Great Northern, Piccadilly & Brompton Railway in 1906, and was opened itself on 11 April 1907, on the site of a former bakery.

The street façade is of the standard shiny red bricks and tiles concealing a steel frame. There are three closely spaced arched windows along Long Acre, above the entrance, and three widely spaced ones along St James's Street above the exit. The 'Arts and Crafts' inspiration behind the detail of the station is still much in evidence, along with the original lifts and their brass controls. The alternative way down to platform level is via a treacherously long spiral staircase.

The station also has a reputation for being the most haunted on the Underground. Even in recent years it seems that staff have had to accept their ghost as part of the job. He is supposed to be the Victorian actor, William Terris, who was stabbed to death by a jealous fellow actor in the Adelphi Theatre in 1897. Quite why he should choose to haunt the station is a matter for speculation – maybe he's waiting for a ghost train!

Ticket window This has tiling with moulded lettering. The Covent Garden ticket windows and other tiling were identical to Green's other stations

Grille above lift door The grille is an 'Arts and Crafts' piece of iron on a tiled frame above number three lift. It is a standard design, also used on Otis lifts supplied to the City & South London in the early 1900s

Platform Advertisements now cover most of the original tiling at platforms like these, which included the station names and elaborate 'Way Out' signs. An individual colour scheme (light brown and yellow in this case) to supplement white was chosen for the tiling along the curved walls and bands across the ceiling

Booking hall tiling The tiling of Green's stations is a distinctive feature throughout. The floral designs inspired by the 'Arts and Crafts' movement on these green tiles have been faithfully copied on the plastic replacements for use during renovation

Lift interior Number three lift, because it is used less frequently than the other two at Covent Garden, has escaped the modern formica panels and advertisements used elsewhere. It is the standard trapezium-shaped lift as supplied to the Group by the Otis Elevator company lined with painted wooden panels

tiles, while the upper part of the arch is painted white. The name of the station is picked out in coloured tiles, forming part of the wall surface. A different colour [scheme] is used for each station, so that habitual passengers on the railway will speedily be able to tell what station they are at without having to look at the name.

The original building at Baker Street was not destined to remain in use. A new booking hall was eventually completed in 1939 within the massive Baker Street station already built by the Metropolitan.

The Great Northern, Piccadilly & Brompton opened in December 1906 just nine months after the Bakerloo. Its stations were at Finsbury Park, Gillespie Road (now Arsenal), Holloway Road, Caledonian Road, York Road (now closed), King's Cross, Russell Square, Holborn, Leicester Square, Piccadilly Circus (shared with the Bakerloo), Dover Street (now Green Park), Down Street (now closed), Hyde Park Corner, Knightsbridge, Brompton Road (now closed), Gloucester Road, Earl's Court, Baron's Court and Hammersmith. At these last two the line ran to the surface and shared platforms with the District. The following year the remaining stations, not then completed, were opened at South Kensington, Covent Garden and Strand (now Aldwych).

In June 1907 the system was completed when the Hampstead line was opened with the following stations: Golders Green, Hampstead, Belsize Park, Chalk Farm, Camden Town, Mornington Crescent, Euston, Euston Road (now Warren Street), Tottenham Court Road (now Goodge Street), Oxford Street (now Tottenham Court Road), Leicester Square (shared with the Piccadilly) and Charing Cross. The line forked at Camden Town, and another branch ran down to join the main line from Highgate (now Archway), Tufnell Park, Kentish Town and South Kentish Town (now closed). The only departure between these and the previous stations was in the use of black lettering on white for the station name.

Almost all Green's stations on these sites remain, including those that have closed (the old booking hall at Hyde Park Corner, for example, now contains a pizza restaurant). The free use of 'Arts and Crafts' décor and the use of glazed blocks for the façades stemmed from ideas long advocated by Halsey Ricardo, who claimed that their self-cleaning qualities and the light and colour they reflected would make London far more attractive. However, later commentators have not been over-generous about Green's efforts. The eminent architectural critic Sir Nikolaus Pevsner wrote in 1942 that 'the feeling for architectural responsibility was there, but with nobody to guide it and nobody to satisfy it according to the highest standards of the day'. Christian Barman, a later publicity officer, was even more scathing, describing the architecture as 'pompous' and continuing '. . . their colour, the colour of ox-liver – about the most unattractive ever used in the streets of London – looks almost black when lit up by the street lamps at night'.

Whatever later reviewers may have said, the buildings certainly stood out in London. This was combined with a more adventurous stance regarding design and publicity – both Harry Ford's 'bullseye' roundel of a solid red circle crossed by a bar (1909) and the adoption of the famous 'UndergrounD' logo being examples. The heart of the Underground was now established.

Several stations on the Yerkes tubes call for special comment. The booking halls at Regent's Park, Trafalgar Square, Oxford Street and Embankment had no new surface buildings, though a visit to Regent's Park will confirm that the interior of the station there was decorated in the same way as those with surface booking halls.

The underground booking hall at Charing Cross, beneath the forecourt of the South Eastern Railway station, was built by excavating the forecourt from above, and this was only allowed after the roof of the main line station had collapsed in December 1905 (killing six people), causing it to be closed for more than three months.

While most stations were supplied with lifts, Gillespie Road, where the station was close to the surface, had none, whereas Finsbury Park (built

Hampstead The black lettering on white for the station names was a feature of stations on the Hampstead line, and a departure from the scheme used for the Bakerloo and Piccadilly Lines

by the Great Northern and leased to the tube line) had two hydraulic lifts to provide interchange with the main line railway, which crossed the road above on a viaduct. The deepest station on the whole network is Hampstead, where the platforms are 192 feet below the surface. This was one of the first stations later equipped with high-speed lifts. A double spiral escalator was installed in a lift shaft at Holloway Road as an experiment, but was never brought into public use.

Golders Green, where the line was built on an embankment, had only steps leading from the brick booking hall to the platforms.

Oxford Street station kept that name for less than a year, when it was combined with the Central London Railway's Tottenham Court Road. The Hampstead Line's Tottenham Court Road was therefore renamed Goodge Street to avoid confusion. The old names of these stations still appear on the platform tunnel walls, though they are largely obscured by posters, as they also do at Marylebone (formerly Great Central station), and Warren Street (formerly Euston Road).

The exterior of the original Holborn station is identical in design to the other Green stations, but was never faced in the glazed blocks, instead being left in white stone. Some other stations, such as Edgware Road, have since had their outsides and/or booking halls painted over.

At its western end, where it met the District, the Piccadilly Line altered its stations at Earl's Court, Baron's Court (built especially to accommodate the new line) and Hammersmith. At Gloucester Road and South Kensington stations of Green's designs were built adjacent to those of the District. The booking hall at Gloucester Road is still in use, but the one at South Kensington has now been converted to house ventilation equipment.

When Gibb retired in 1910 his place was taken by the naturalized American, Albert Stanley, whom Gibb had coaxed over in 1907. Stanley was at first general manager and later managing director of the Underground Group, becoming chairman in 1919. He continued in this capacity until 1947, long after the Group became London Transport in 1933. He was knighted in 1914, and was to become Lord Ashfield in 1920.

The three tube companies were amalgamated into the London Electric Railway, and Stanley began to consider what extensions would be most useful. Independent expansion was abandoned for the time being as too much initial investment would

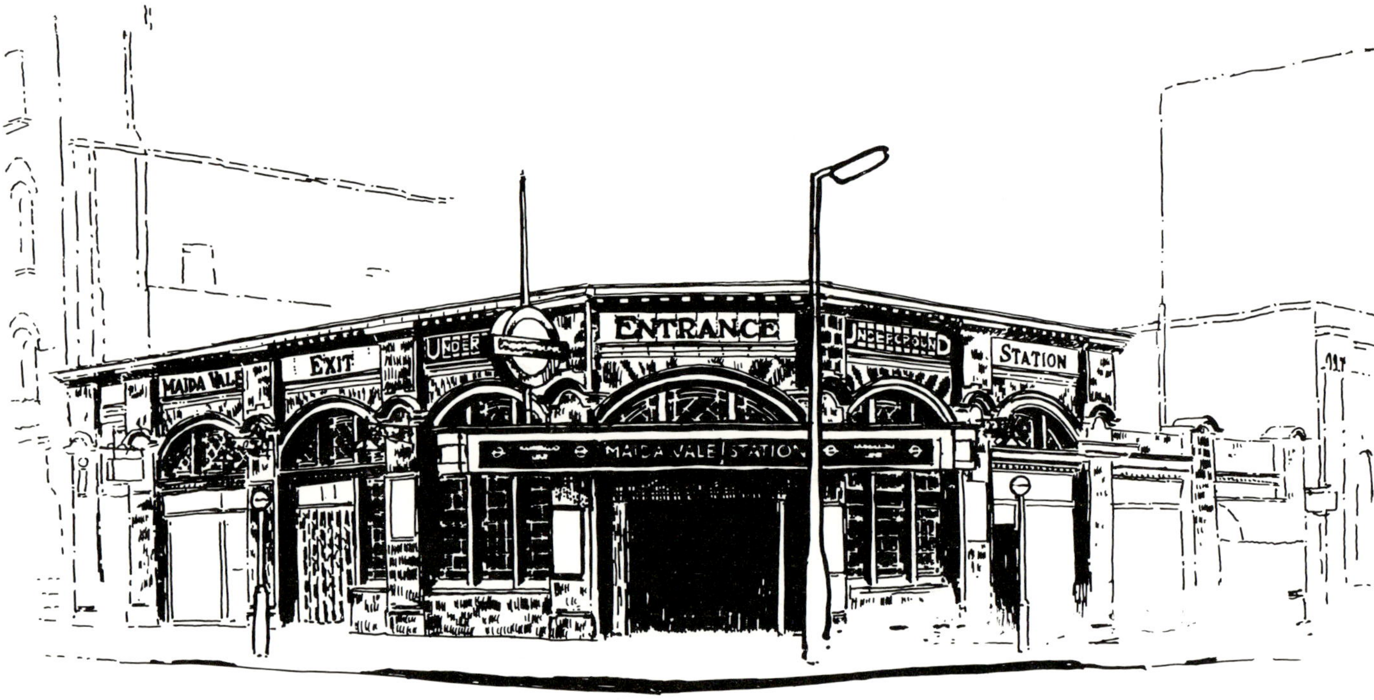

Maida Vale A later development after the style of Leslie Green. Its sister station at Kilburn Park is now a listed building

be needed, so the first stage of a development to link the Bakerloo to the London & North Western Railway was the only plan pursued.

New stations were opened at Paddington (1913) and at Warwick Avenue, Maida Vale and Kilburn Park (1915). Paddington was built with a sub-surface booking hall, entered by a subway entrance of glazed red blocks on the north side of Praed Street, opposite the Metropolitan station. Warwick Avenue also had the booking hall underground, but the other two gained surface buildings with red-glazed exteriors. These buildings differed from the earlier ones. Their single storeys were not so tall, and the arches over the windows became flattened. Lettering outside the stations was on white blocks. As before, design work was in Leslie Green's style but inside they all looked quite different from his original stations. Green himself had been made an Associate of the Royal Institute of British Architects in 1899, and he became a Fellow in 1907 after his work for both the Yerkes tubes and the District. On 31 August 1908 he died suddenly, only thirty-three years old, and the architects' department had to continue without him.

At Kilburn Park the booking hall was in the surface building, which is now Department of the Environment listed. When entering the building at Maida Vale, however, one descends a flight of stairs to reach the booking hall. The high interior walls are faced with mosaics of the bullseye and UndergrounD devices, while

Booking hall interior, Maida Vale The decorative scheme at this station and its contemporaries saw a departure from the earlier 'Arts and Crafts' floral motifs

lower down liberal use was made of bands of small chequered tiles. The wooden central ticket booth was to become a standard feature in new Underground stations until the 1930s. The chequered tiles were continued at the other stations, and none of them was fitted with lifts, as the original mouldings at the ends of the escalator shafts testify. At the foot of the escalators at each of these stations was a cross-connection immediately between the platforms – a pattern also followed at later stations. The platform décor at the four stations was simpler than Green's earlier ones, as the walls were just faced in white tiling with coloured edging, varied at each location.

In the same year that Warwick Avenue, Maida Vale and Kilburn Park were opened, so were new platforms at Queen's Park. This was an old London & North Western Railway station, built in 1879 (the entrance was modified in the late 1970s) as part of the agreement with that company. Trains also ran on to Willesden Junction, and in 1916 the L & NWR opened a new station between the two at Kensal Green especially for the new tube trains. From 1917 the Bakerloo operated a through service all the way to Watford Junction via Watford High Street, Bushey (& Oxhey), Carpenders Park, (Pinner &) Hatch End, Headstone Lane, Harrow & Wealdstone, Kenton, North Wembley, Wembley for Sudbury (later Wembley Central), Stonebridge Park and Harlesden. Most of these stations had been either built or reconstructed between 1911 and 1913. Watford Junction had a sprawling, single-storey brick building with a clock tower, and Watford High Street was constructed with a recessed entrance. Headstone Lane, Kenton, North Wembley, Stonebridge Park and Harlesden all possess identical unremarkable small, square-brick buildings with 'pyramid' roofs, Willesden Junction having a larger building in the same style. Each was either situated by the tracks or on a bridge over them. The stations on the line at Kensal Green, Wembley and Carpenders Park have all since been rebuilt, and an extra station was built at South Kenton in 1933. The three stations so far not dealt with, at Bushey & Oxhey, Pinner & Hatch End, and Harrow & Wealdstone, differed from the other L & NWR stations because they were rebuilt earlier on

Harrow & Wealdstone This building, constructed by the LNWR in 1897, was served by Underground trains and main line suburban services from 1917

the sites of former stations belonging to the London & Birmingham Railway erected in the 1840s. The L & NWR reconstructed stations date from 1897 and are much more ostentatious than those built fifteen years later. The ornate brick and stone façade at Harrow & Wealdstone is an example. Each station was built with a clock tower and weathervane, the company's initials being carved out along the top of the building.

The L & NWR was very enthusiastic about the whole scheme from the start, and the tube trains for the through service to Elephant & Castle were jointly owned, being painted in the main line company's colours of sepia and white. It planned to run its own electric trains on the new track into its terminus at Euston, but this part of the plan was delayed until 1922 because of the First World War. Its new station at Kensal Green was until then only served by tube trains.

On 1 January 1913 the City & South London and Central London Railways were transferred to the Underground Group. An extension to the Central London was planned under similar terms to that of the Bakerloo extension. The Ealing & Shepherd's Bush Railway was to be built by the Great Western to connect Ealing Broadway to its West London Railway. After deliberation it was decided to link this line to that of the Central London north of Wood Lane, which was being revamped with Underground motifs. A through service of tube trains could then run to Ealing Broadway. Work on the line continued throughout the war, and the tube service began in 1920 with a new intermediate station at East Acton. Two more stations, at North Acton and West Acton, were added in 1923, and the original brick buildings survive at two.

A curious feature of the line was the flyover, still in use today, between East Acton and Wood Lane. It will be recalled that Wood Lane was built on a loop from Shepherd's Bush, but to try to minimize the curve between the two stations, which are at right-angles to one another, the trains ran around the loop and through Wood Lane in an anticlockwise direction. They then continued under the original line and back to Shepherd's Bush. When leads were taken off the loop it was consequently found that trains ran on the right, rather than left as was standard practice. The flyover, where the westbound line crosses the eastbound, was constructed to remedy the situation before the tube trains reached the shared tracks with the Great Western. In later years the station built at White City, replacing Wood Lane, had to adapt to the odd layout, and the traveller today will find his train on the left side of the station at East Acton, on the right at White City, and back on the left again at Shepherd's Bush!

The Central London Railway terminus was the old Great Western station at Ealing Broadway, built in 1838. It was a typical early Great Western station, with its short,

East Acton A modest little booking hall, with platforms, was constructed here next to the GWR line, to serve CLR trains bound for Ealing Broadway from 1920

Ealing Broadway This was the old GWR station, which served as a terminus for the CLR from 1920 until its extensive reconstruction in 1966, when the District Line entrance was transferred from its adjacent site

sloped towers tiled and crowned with ornate iron railings; stations similar to this were found all along Brunel's railway. By the time the tube arrived large wooden sign-boards, like those at other stations, almost obscured the upper half of the building. To the left of it a row of shops had been built, above which was a sign advertising a 'frequent service of Central London Electric Trains to West End and City'. The platforms for the Central are still in use today, with their serrated valanced canopies, but the station building was entirely rebuilt in 1966, when a new combined entrance for British Rail and Central and District trains was opened. The District Railway building next door was closed at the same time.

By the 1920s all the Underground railways were under the control of the same group – all, that is, except the Metropolitan, which valued its independence too highly. The way lay open for new station designs on proposed extensions by both parties, and for the next decade experimentation became the keyword as the 'Underground' concept grew stronger.

3 The Evolution of Corporate Identity

At the start of the 1920s the character of the Underground Group was being radically altered. With the basis of today's network firmly established a halt had been called in the building of entirely new lines, and the trend towards expanding and integrating the system gained more emphasis. How much expansion was due to the need to serve new commuters and how much was triggered off by the Group itself more rightly belongs in a study of the Underground as an instrument of social change. Some idea may nevertheless be gained by the Metropolitan's hard sell of 'Metro-land', and by the fact that when the Hampstead line's northern terminus at Golders Green was built the station stood in open country, but was soon surrounded by housing developments. The fact remains that all station construction was to be restricted to extensions and modernization programmes for more than forty years hence. No completely new Underground railway would be built in London until the Victoria Line in the 1960s.

The demand for improvement in public transport facilities, which was to result in the 1933 formation of the London Passenger Transport Board, left the bus, tram and rail operators of the 1920s much to do to attract custom. The first major creation of the Underground was an extension of the Hampstead line from the open-air station at Golders Green. This station had had a small additional brick entrance with a sloping roof from Finchley Road, opened in 1911, and a plastered white entrance was added now to the existing brick buildings.

In November 1923 two stations were opened, at Brent (now Brent Cross) and Hendon Central, the first new custom-built surface stations to be used by tube train extensions. At platform level the stations were not very different from other suburban stations before them. A single island platform was constructed between the tracks, covered by a shallow gabled wood and glass canopy with scalloped valances. Outside, they were specifically designed to fit in with the new developing commuter areas north of London.

Hendon Central One of Heaps' first stations for the Group, Hendon Central opened in 1923; the surrounding façade was added soon after the opening date

Stanley Heaps, the organization's chief architect, was responsible for the designs of the stations on the new branch. The entrances to them were through a series of stone columns, and although Brent was a smaller detached building, the façade at Hendon Central was to be extended upwards and outwards to a building which cut across the corner of Central Circus, between Watford Way and Queens Road. The classical lines of this building, though simplified, were planned to fit in with new commuter developments, and the mock-Georgian style was later adapted to two other stations on the branch. The station name was made up of individual letters fixed directly to the stone canopy, above which ran a simply decorated wrought iron railing. The booking office was adorned with rectangular white glazed tiles with black and green edging – the standard interior decoration for the Group until about 1930.

In August 1924 the line reached what was to become its northern terminus at Edgware, with an intermediate station opened at Colindale. The station between these, Burnt Oak, was not completed until two months later. Both Colindale and Burnt Oak followed Brent in having a relatively small station building, and the platforms remained the same. It has been said that only the absence of chimney stacks made the stations different from the houses that surrounded them, and there is some truth in this. But Burnt Oak gives some idea of the direction in which the Underground was moving, for it appears a far more functional building than those built within the decade by the Metropolitan, on its branches to Watford and Stanmore. The façade of Burnt Oak is delightfully simple, having an extended lower portion flanked on either side by flat-roofed shops. The front elevation of the upper floor has three windows, with stone set into the brickwork, and the whole is crowned by a pyramidal tiled roof with wide, projecting eaves. A period innovation stands on the wall in front of the station (which continues across the bridge over the tracks). This is the three-dimensional representation of the Group's 'UndergrounD' bar-and-circle, developed from the earlier

Burnt Oak Opened in 1924, this was the last station completed on the Edgware branch. It represents a meeting point of surface ornamentation and a more functional outlook

Edgware The most bizarre station on the branch was constructed at Edgware. This northern terminus was built in an 'Italian' style

bullseye device. It is raised clear of the wall on an iron stand, pierced vertically by a white staff. The idea was to make the station stand out for what it was, and the device was subsequently added to both old and new stations as a unifying piece of design.

The publicity brochure concerned with the opening of the line definitely describes the above stations as being of Georgian appearance. The terminus at Edgware, however, took the idea to extremes. The tiled roof was maintained, but the station was to be altogether more 'Italian in feeling'. Indeed, when completed it ended up looking more like a Roman villa than the access point to a modern electric railway! The front elevation showed liberal use of Portland stone and brickwork, fronted by a Doric colonnade. The eastern wing consisted of shops separated by columns, whereas the western wing was to provide shelter and a waiting room for bus passengers, for in 1912 the London General Omnibus Company had been taken over by the Underground Group. The station was therefore specially designed to facilitate easy interchange with the buses, and formed one of the first purpose-built bus and rail termini. Corresponding with the social habits prevailing at the time, prospective commuters were provided with a cycle shed with space for a hundred machines.

Inside Edgware Station one finds the same tiling pattern prevalent at other stations on the extension. The station is adjacent to the depot, and the platforms on this side (numbers 2 and 3) are covered by a high curved roof. The stair passage to platform 1 is a fairly recent addition, but apart from this the station remains much as built, except for removal of the western wing.

The extension to Edgware was the first stage in a major project to unite and expand the Hampstead and City & South London tubes, forming the Northern Line. The Hampstead line was to be continued southwards under the Embankment and Thames to Waterloo and Kennington, while the City & South London would be linked with the former at Camden Town. This should have provided a variety of possible through routes, but one major obstacle barred this relatively simple exercise. It will be recalled that all the tubes constructed after the City & South London had been built with marginally wider tunnels. If this older railway was to accommodate standard tube rolling stock then the tunnels would have to be widened. The nature of the 'tube' railway forbade any diversion of the trains on this route, so the whole length of it was closed, in stages, between 1922 and 1924. The opportunity was taken at the same time to carry out reconstruction work on the station exteriors as well as interiors. It is here that Frank Pick and Charles Holden begin their involvement in our story.

Frank Pick's career in underground railways spanned over thirty years. He had been brought in by Sir George Gibb, whom he had served as personal assistant with the North Eastern Railway, when Gibb was appointed by the Group in 1906. He continued in a junior post under Albert Stanley, but his persistent dissatisfaction first with publicity and then with general aspects of the service was most vocal. In 1909 Stanley made him traffic officer, with responsibility for advertising, and in 1912, commercial manager. After a short time at the Board of Trade, Pick then became joint assistant managing director (1921), then managing director (1928). From the formation of 'London Transport' in 1933 until his retirement in 1940 he was vice-chairman under Stanley (by then Lord Ashfield). His overriding enthusiasm for excellence in design and presentation during his career resulted in the further evolution of the UndergrounD roundel, as well as the typeface of Edward Johnston used to this day for publicity and other purposes. The schematic, rather than geographical, map of the Underground (which has been referred to as one of the greatest feats of graphic design this century) emerged in the early 1930s, and posters were commissioned by leading artists such as McKnight Kauffer and Sutherland. Standardization under his term of office reached right down to such everyday objects as bus stops and litter bins.

Pick's interest in design was not just in pursuance of better images, for he sought to combine them into a corporate identity. The stations on the Edgware extension did not really look as 'Underground' stations should, but although Pick knew something different was needed he was not quite sure what. In most things his skill lay in knowing who to commission to produce what he himself did not have the expertise to do, so with the impending reconstruction of the City & South London stations and an extension southwards to Morden planned, he began to search for a new spirit. The man he eventually selected to work with Heaps was Charles Holden.

Holden was a respected architect, whom Pick had first met at a European manufacturers' exhibition in the City in 1915. When Pick invited him to work on the new projects he was delighted to have the freedom

Side entrance at Westminster This is significant as it appears to have been Charles Holden's first commission from the Group

EMBANKMENT

Embankment entrance This is a matching entrance with the one in Villiers Street, connected by a through arcade. On the left is the Hungerford Bridge carrying the British Rail lines into the Southern Railway's Charing Cross station. There are also steps to the pedestrian walkway across the bridge

Staircase down to District Line The tiling and colour scheme of the new 1920s station was continued throughout staircases and connecting tunnels

Embankment station is one of several on the Underground to have gone through intermittent name changes in its long history. The original District Line station opened in 1870 as Charing Cross, and was constructed over typical cut-and-cover tunnels built into the new Victoria Embankment. The Bakerloo station of 1906 was called Embankment, and altered to Charing Cross (Embankment) when the Hampstead line terminus platform and reversing loop were added in 1914. The following year the combined stations became Charing Cross.

The plan to extend the Hampstead line southwards in the early 1920s, in order to link up with the old City & South London at Kennington to form the Northern Line, led to the removal of the loop. This was replaced by a new platform for southbound traffic below Villiers Street, the old platform being retained for northbound traffic. This was completed by 1926, when a major reconstruction programme for the station was begun to improve passenger facilities. Congestion in the old layout led to a new, larger booking hall being built next to the arcade connecting the Villiers Street and Embankment entrances. A concourse was built below the District platforms to make a convenient interchange between the three lines, and new staircases and escalators (the first used at a sub-surface station layout) were constructed. Interior décor was of the white, rectangular tiling, with green and black, used in contemporary renovation programmes. This unified the new interior elements, the old Bakerloo/Hampstead platforms remaining as built.

Further minor improvements were made to the station for the Festival of Britain in 1951.

The station was renamed Charing Cross Embankment in 1974, and again just Embankment in 1976 in preparation for the opening of the Jubilee extension to Charing Cross station in the Strand.

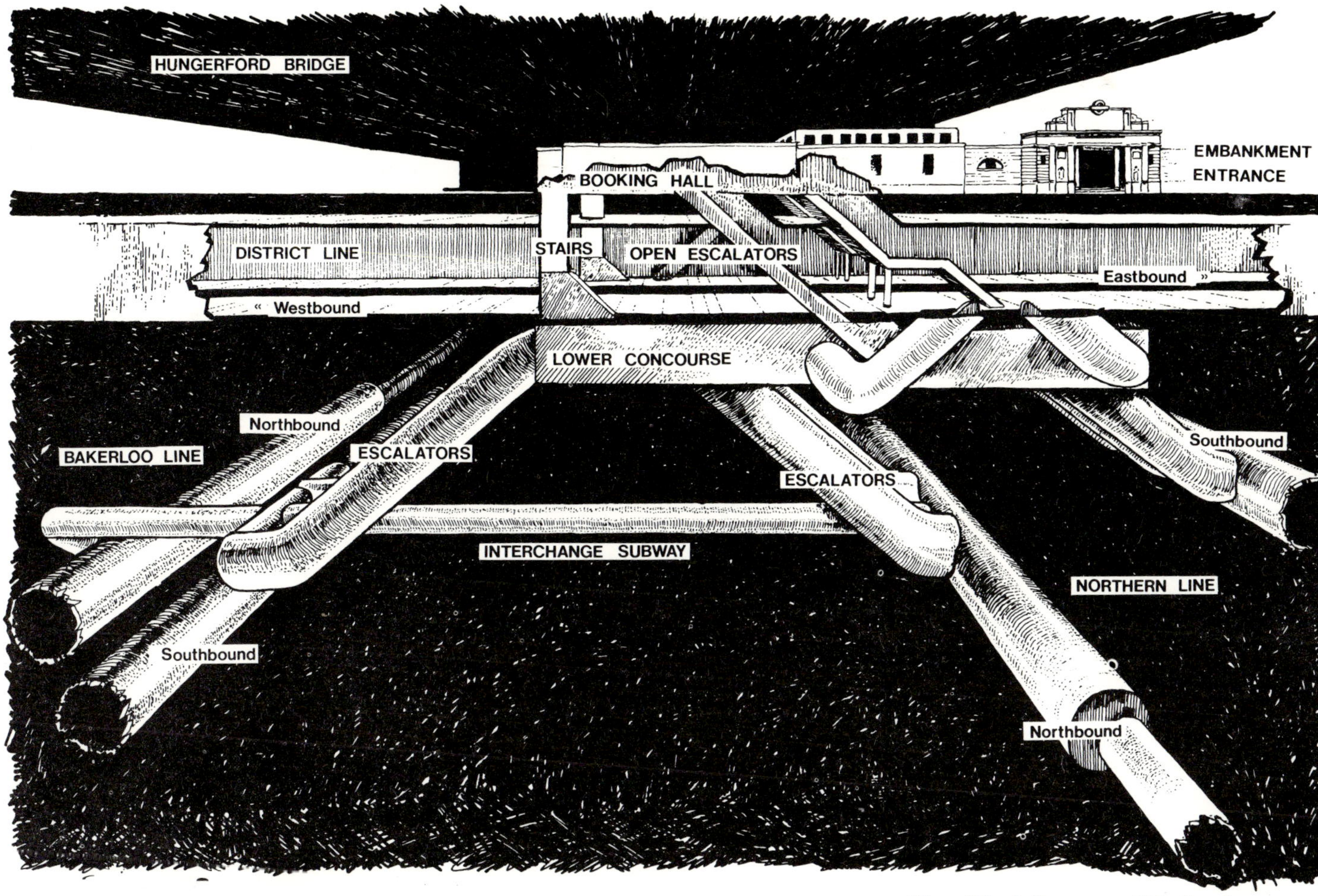

Simplified diagram of Embankment station This was the new station layout after the substantial 1920s reconstruction, before further work in 1950. The difference in construction and level between the cut-and-cover District and the tube Bakerloo and Northern Lines is very marked. The two tubes run southward here under the River Thames to Waterloo

Northern Line southbound platform As a more recent platform, this does not conform to the standard décor of the older Bakerloo and northbound Northern platforms. Standard 1920s tiling was applied to all new or modernized Northern Line platforms

Cross-section of the Victoria Embankment This shows the pipes, sewers and tunnels, and on the left the District Line tunnel. They were all built into the new embankment. Apart from these, the Victoria Embankment was built to form a new road between Westminster and the City. The River Thames is on the right

Oval If this is compared with the earlier view of Oval, a great change will be apparent. Most old CSLR stations were altered in this manner by Holden

to experiment with more radical architecture than he had been working on until then. Arrangements were therefore made with his firm, Adams, Holden & Pearson, to try something small at first.

Opinions vary on what Holden's first station was, for Bond Street has been dated 1924. Its features were more in keeping with some later reconstructions, such as Holborn (1932-3), but it has since been remodelled to accommodate the Jubilee Line. It seems likely that the small back entrance to the District station at Westminster, which was being rebuilt, was Holden's trial commission.
A simple flat white slab, with minimal decoration, was the result. Few could have foreseen that this would prove such a landmark, for Holden would eventually design stations that are widely regarded as among the best British architecture of the age. For the moment, however, his influence grew slowly.

Pick's enthusiasm for Holden allowed the board to appoint him to work on modernizing the stations at Oval, Stockwell, Clapham North and Clapham Common as well as the others on the City & South London. Borough, for example, received a new façade of cream slabs, as did Clapham North. Inside, the booking halls and platforms were given standard tiling. Oval was refaced in cream with random black chips, but although parts of the old brickwork can be seen at some stations their character became submerged under the modern influence. Clapham Common was perhaps more successful, for here a domed subway entrance faced in the cream slabs leads down to an underground booking hall.

The island platforms at Clapham Common, Clapham North and Angel assumed their present form as part of this programme, though that at Angel has more recently been adapted for use by the blind (the Royal National Institute for the Blind being nearby). This has involved grooved paving slabs in the centre of the platforms, extra guard rails on the seats, and extra wide raised white lines at the edge. There was also an island platform at Euston, which was converted into an extra wide single platform when the station was reconstructed to accommodate the Victoria Line in the 1960s.

It would probably be fair to say that stations such as these, where Holden worked on existing buildings, were not as successful architecturally as those where he was in a position to design brand new station buildings. The complex intertwined junction at Camden Town, between the Hampstead line and the former 'sardine box railway' opened in 1924, and in 1926 the southern version at Kennington was added. Embankment and Waterloo had been substantially reconstructed, but the innovative part of the line was the new extension to Morden, opened at the same time, for which Holden had designed the stations at Clapham South, Balham, Trinity Road (now Tooting Bec), Tooting

Island platform, Angel Even after refurbishing several old CSLR stations retained 'island' platforms

Broadway, Collier's Wood, South Wimbledon and Morden itself.

Holden devised the idea of a three-leafed folding screen dominated by a large window following this shape. The idea was to form a standard design that could be adapted to fit whatever site was chosen for the station, and the angles between the walls could be widely varied. The booking halls were placed below ground level with the platforms – reached by escalators – between them, but it was the surface buildings that were so revolutionary. There was great scope for Holden to experiment, in particular with lighting effects. A full-sized mock-up of the first station to be built to this pattern – at Clapham South – was constructed at the engineering works at Earl's Court so that various arrangements could be tried. Pick brushed aside any opposition from the board and wrote gleefully about the modern designs, the lack of ornaments, how everything was subservient to the doorway – a 'hole in the wall' – and a notice about what it was. He concluded: '. . . in order that I may go mad in good company I have got Holden to see that we do it properly.' At the same time he kept reminding Holden to keep in sight the total effect of his new stations; for example, although poster space may not be planned it might one day be needed. The architect was asked to bear this in mind now, '. . . rather than that it should be patched later'.

Trinity Road (renamed Tooting Bec in 1950) showed the typical surface building arrangement. There were two entrances on opposite sides of the road junction, one of which was angled so acutely to fit the site that the 'holes in the wall' were moved a considerable distance back from the apex. All elevations at these stations are of Portland stone – Holden's favourite material. For optimum lighting the windows

Tooting Bec Opened as Trinity Road in 1926, this entrance is a typical example of the 'Morden' style used by Holden on that extension

Morden At the southern terminus of the line the three-leaf screen symbolically became a flat façade. The upper storeys were added to the station building at a later date

are large, with vertical glazing bars which blend in perfectly, and featuring the UndergrounD roundel in the centre. Above the windows and entrances ran flat blue canopies bearing the station name and carrying external floodlighting. The pillars dividing the leaves show Holden's only concession to ornament, for they are surmounted by spheres pierced by slabs in a three-dimensional representation of the Group's symbol.

The exteriors of these new stations were not the only areas intended to be lacking in subtlety, as the entrances led down to sub-surface booking halls. To retain the basic approach Holden eventually decided on a chandelier of exposed light bulbs to illuminate the inside of his new buildings at night. At Clapham South he had been able to design a hexagonal ticket hall, owing to the shape of the site, but the escalators to platform level had to approach the line at right-angles. It was therefore decided to create an extra-long concourse between the platforms in order to give two-way access to them, and as a result the running tunnels here are further apart than elsewhere on the line.
It was with these stations that the Underground became something of an innovator, for it seems that Pick was more interested in giving the public what he thought was best for them – an exciting new approach with no half measures. The way was paved towards public acceptance of modern architecture, for there later followed a proliferation of shops, factories and other public buildings all based on the same ideal. The passage of time has been unkind to these buildings, if only because plain white stone loses its attractiveness when it becomes dirty. It is difficult for us today to appreciate the new style appearing at that time in Britain, but it is probably fair to say that many buildings of the 1920s and 1930s, such as the well-known Hoover factory in West London, have a period charm. Their art deco decoration is attractive, but these simple stations of Holden's are somehow less dated.

Morden station was the end of the line and, just as the folding screen had been taken to an extreme at one of the Trinity Road entrances, the opposite arrangement was adopted here. The screen was opened out to form a flat front perpendicular to the line of the tracks, and the building continued at a lower level for

Interior of Morden This is a view from the footbridge above the platforms, showing the destination indicator and tiling pattern. The roof was the last of its kind ever built by the Underground

Chandelier at Morden Functionalism on the Morden line was extended to such items as light fittings, designed to be as basic as possible

some distance on either side, to be occupied by shops. The stations on the line were designed on the same principle as that of Leslie Green – that is, they could have extra storeys added. The addition of offices over Morden occurred much later, and as with so many stations of this type is of an inferior design standard with little regard for the original building. The main portion of the exterior forms a large empty box – a sort of antechamber – which could be used by people waiting for buses. The next area within is the booking hall, where the wooden ticket booth is placed directly below a polygonal skylight – a common feature at the other stations. Proceeding further through, one comes to a series of bridges and stairways that lead to the central island platform and two flanking platforms below. Tiling throughout is standard, but the station differs from the others because here the line runs up to the surface and the platforms lie in a cutting. The interior layout is therefore a familiar one, the whole thing being covered by a wide roof with a shallow arch, supported by girders and similar to that at Edgware. The major difference between these roofs and older ones such as Earl's Court is that the roof profile can be flatter and built without vents, for of course the earlier ones were built to accommodate steam trains

PICCADILLY CIRCUS

Ironwork around subway entrance Designed and erected by the local authority, these railings have become a familiar sight to the London tourist, who will readily associate them with an image of the capital

Holden's Piccadilly Circus reconstruction got under way with the building of a mock-up of the booking hall in the engineering workships at Earl's Court. The hall was to lic underneath the statue of Eros, with subway entrances radiating out around Nash's original Circus. The booking hall was to feature a parade of shops around its nearly elliptical perimeter, lit by lanterns fixed atop the supporting columns. Holden chose materials of the highest quality – red scagliola for the columns, bronze for fitments, and Travertine marble. The construction of the new hall was completed in 1928, and was immediately heralded as a masterpiece of modern architectural design.

The open subway entrances originally had temporary timber panels around the opening, which Holden designed with a simple 'stepped' appearance. These were replaced by the railings in place today, which were provided by the local administration rather than by the Underground. There were also entrances from the old Leslie Green booking hall and another leading direct to the Swan & Edgar department store between Piccadilly and Regent Street, which had display windows on the subway approach. The ticket machines, delivered shortly after the opening of the reconstructed station, were of a new shorter design which fitted in well with the new hall.

Time has not been kind to Holden's Piccadilly Circus, for the removal of the original lighting and the arbitrary positioning of many items has to a great extent destroyed the atmosphere of the station. Currently there are plans afoot to redecorate Piccadilly Circus, which may perhaps restore some order to what has become a renowned London landmark.

Booking hall Despite the general clutter it is still possible to visualize the way Holden saw the station. Among the shops around the edge is an information desk next to display panels that are used to publicize items of general interest concerning London Transport

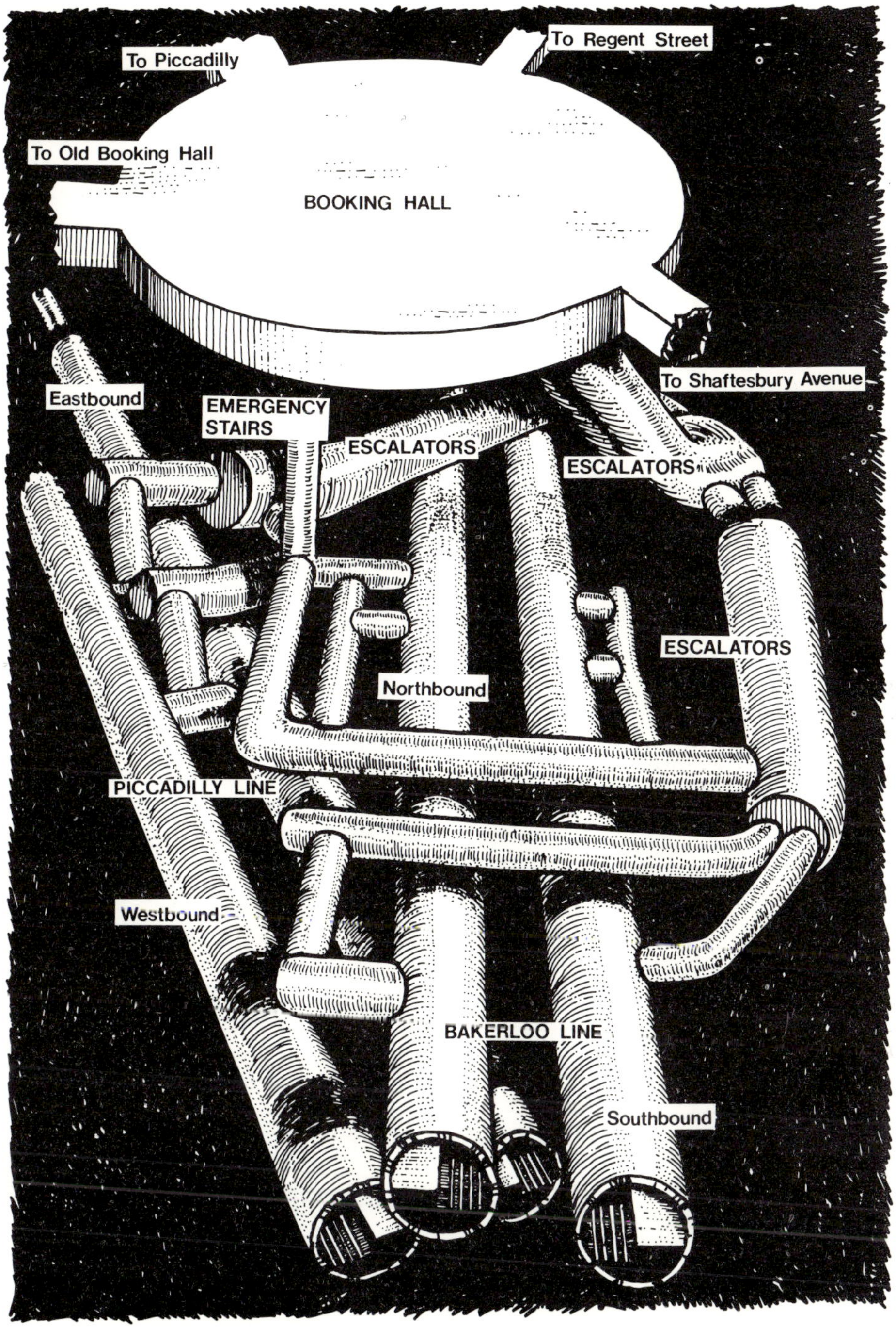

Simplified diagram of Piccadilly Circus station Reconstruction work involved the inclusion of a main bank of five escalators to an intermediate level, where separate escalator shafts led to the two tube lines. In addition, deep-level interconnecting passages were constructed so that passengers could be directed along different routes going to and from the platforms. This formed an impressive concealed labyrinth below ground

Deep-level connections to Bakerloo Line At the foot of the Bakerloo's escalator the passageway forks to each platform. Although these passageways were decorated with standard 1920s tiling, the décor of the original platforms was left untouched

55 BROADWAY/ ST JAMES'S PARK

Exterior The building itself received highly favourable critical reaction when it was completed in 1929, and 55 Broadway is now regarded as one of the most successful commercial London buildings of the 1920s

Holden's design for St James's Park station, the Group's headquarters, was based on an ingenious cruciform arrangement. The building had a mostly plain stone exterior stepped up to a tower. As with Piccadilly Circus, the interior was sumptuously decorated with the extensive use of expensive materials, and the lighting and supporting columns in the booking hall were completed in the same manner. This hall also featured a solid marble base for the ticket booth, which was the only one of its kind (others having simulated marble sheets pasted on to the timber frame). Away from the public gaze were open plan offices for the Underground staff. All fitments were designed personally by Holden, including lamp standards and the furniture of the senior executives' offices. This was encouraged by Frank Pick, who had long admired the total design efforts of architects such as Charles Rennie Mackintosh.

High on the outside of the building were eight sculptures, representing the four winds. Among the artists commissioned to produce these were Eric Gill, Eric Aumonier and Henry Moore, who had only just become a professional sculptor. Further down the building, at first floor level, were two sculptures by Jacob Epstein entitled 'Night' and 'Day'. These outraged the press, as had his sculptures adorning Holden's 1908 BMA building in the Strand, from which they were later removed when the building was acquired by the Rhodesian Government. The Board was under pressure to remove Epstein's pieces; Pick argued Holden's case for keeping them even though he had already remarked in 1925 that he was '. . . thoroughly tired of Epstein's ugly women!' When Holden was later appointed architect to the new London University buildings he was instructed that under no circumstances should Epstein be allowed near them!

Platforms The station platforms were decorated with standard 1920s tiling and retained the old destination indicators. Recently experiments have been carried out with a computerized display that also shows the expected waiting times for each train

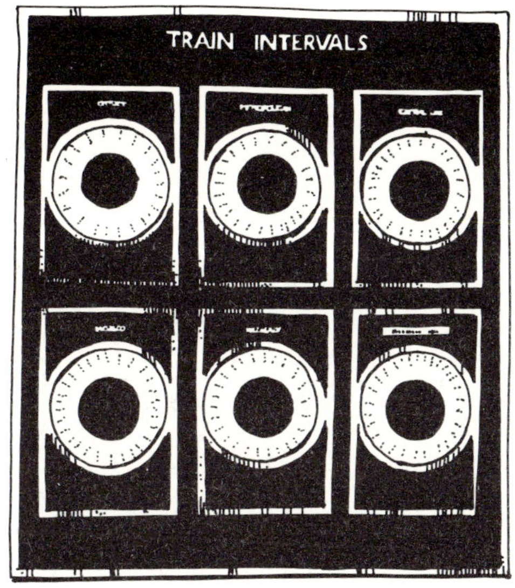

Interval clocks This panel of six clocks shows the interval running times on the lines associated with the Group when the station was reconstructed, and so does not display information on the Victoria or Jubilee Lines

'Day' sculpture The single action that saved the sculptures occurred when Epstein was persuaded to climb up to 'Day' and set about reducing in size the obvious masculinity of the little boy

'Night' sculpture When Epstein's sculptures were unveiled they were widely criticized. 'Night' became the subject of nocturnal attacks with such weapons as paint and 'tar bombs'

Warren Street The continued use of Portland stone for stations in town resulted in this curved façade, designed by Heaps, the staff architect

requiring a route for the rising steam to escape. When Holden next designed open-air terminal stations the somewhat cluttered roof design would have disappeared completely.

Pick was delighted with the stations on the Morden Line, and this was revealed in the brochure he wrote for the opening of the line:

> The design is of no particular school; it neither apes the past nor underlines modernity by violating taste. It is an attempt to show the purpose of the building in a manner combining simplicity and strength with grace and character . . . The Public should have no difficulty in recognizing an Underground station.

Pick's concern for total design also led to an irritated disclaimer below a diagram of Tooting Broadway:

> P.S. – The Underground Railway is not responsible for the placing of the three maimed trees that obstruct the footwalk outside this station.

On Pick's initiative, Holden agreed that the idea of a basement level booking hall would be ideal for any reconstruction of stations in the centre of town. The natural target for the first of these was Leslie Green's Piccadilly Circus, which was ridiculously congested, though there was no way to expand the original booking hall laterally; it had already been made larger than the standard hall of Green's stations. It stood on the corner of Piccadilly and Haymarket, and was approached from entrances on three sides. In order to speed up traffic flow it had already been decided to replace the lifts with escalators, in common with other stations, but as major rebuilding would be necessary for this Pick instructed Holden to transform the station completely. The work was placed for the first time under the direct control of Adams, Holden & Pearson, and was completed in 1928. The old building remained in use as a subway entrance and others were added around the Circus, all leading to a round booking hall directly below the centre. The finishings were carried out in quality materials and the station was widely praised for both its functional and its aesthetic qualities.

Once work had started at Piccadilly Circus, Holden's attention turned to the station at St James's Park, which was also the headquarters of the Group. It had already been partially rebuilt, but the site offered to Holden was regarded as too awkward to be of any value. He developed instead a clever cruciform idea, which would occupy a larger site but would allow access to the station incorporated in the building from both the Broadway and Petty France sides. This would form a passage that could bisect at right-angles to the main axis of the building. Not for the first time Pick rushed the plans past the Board, and work began almost immediately. The new building has frequently been praised, but when it was completed in 1929 the press were outraged by the sculptures that adorned it – particularly those by Jacob Epstein. Nonetheless, 55 Broadway remains one of the most important buildings of that time.

Several other stations in the centre of London were rebuilt with the Portland stone screen from the

Bank This subway entrance, one of a number around the Central Line booking hall, is actually part of the corner of the Bank of England itself

late 1920s through the 1930s, initially from Holden's sketches but with most of the work by Heaps. Leicester Square was redesigned and rebuilt between 1930 and 1935 on similar lines to Piccadilly Circus, with entrances based on the 'Morden' design on the corners of Cranbourn Street and Charing Cross Road, and the latter and Little Newport Street. Elsewhere on the Piccadilly Line, Down Street was closed and the nearby station at Dover Street became Green Park in 1933. The underground booking hall here was reached from an isolated low Portland stone building on the north side of the park, which also acted as a bus shelter. Mansion House (on the District) and Knightsbridge (1934) gained screen façades on corner sites, while others had a flat stone elevation. Both Bond Street and Marble Arch (the latter dates from 1932) on the Central are of this type, as is the new entrance provided at Holborn. In 1933 the old Central London station at British Museum was closed and a new interchange with the Piccadilly was provided at Holborn – the rebuilding dates from this time. In 1929 the sub-surface booking hall at Post Office (now St Paul's) was altered, and other underground halls without surface buildings followed at Chancery Lane, Hyde Park Corner and Monument. The last named was opened in 1935.

Bank Station (Central Line) was reconstructed during the major rebuilding of the Bank of England, which began in 1925. When work was completed the sub-surface booking hall had been redecorated and was reached by a number of subway entrances, including one built into the corner of the Bank itself.

From 1933 the Metropolitan Railway and the other Underground lines were under the control of the same body, and Euston Square could also be rebuilt. Nearby, the old Warren Street station on the Hampstead line was transformed by Heaps. The Portland stone façade was altered into a semi-circular pattern within which lay the booking hall; the building was extended upwards and behind to form 'Warren Court'. The inside of this station is nowadays a curious mixture. The upper levels of passages were redecorated when the Victoria Line was built, and below these are the escalators dating from Heaps' reconstruction. The Northern Line platforms remain as built, with

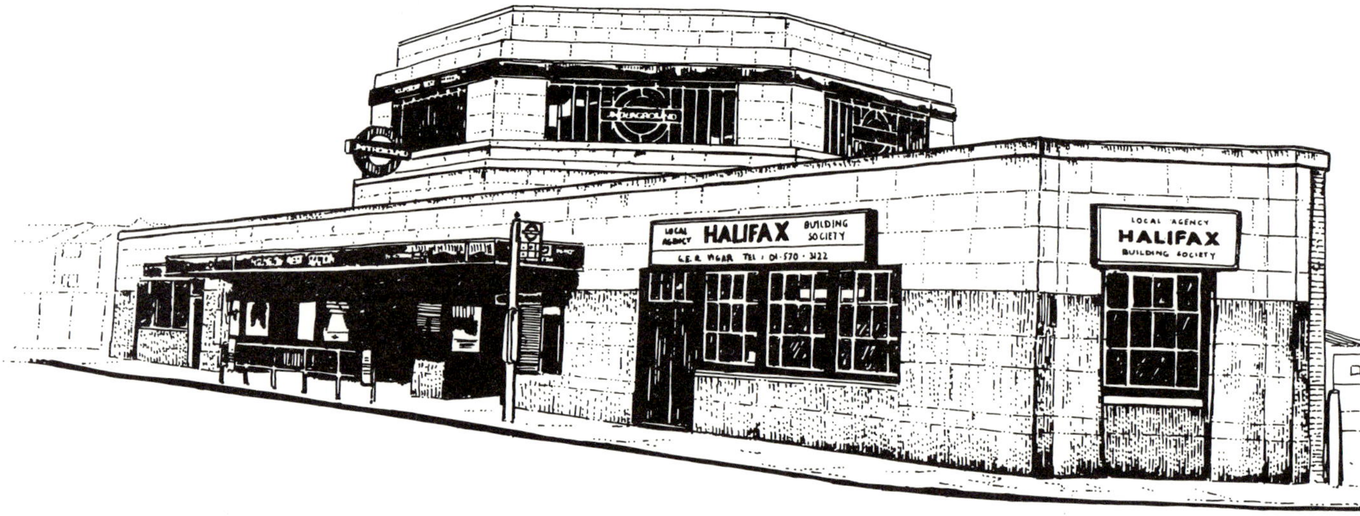

Hounslow West The last developments of the 'Morden' style, both Hounslow West and its sister station at Ealing Common retained the use of Portland stone

portions of the original name – 'Euston Road' – still visible. Much of the rebuilding work at the time, including Holden's Piccadilly Circus, left the original platforms of Green's stations untouched. Elsewhere interior surfaces were at first covered with the standard tiles. They were not really in keeping with the spirit sought by Holden and Pick, but at the time such menial details were left to other departments and Holden did not have responsibility for this. The first appearance of square, matt-glazed, biscuit-coloured tiles had been in the subways leading to the booking hall at Piccadilly Circus, and Holden was later to make this his standard interior design feature, once Pick had ensured that Holden was in charge of everything. Platforms at Holborn, for example, have the later tiles.

For some time plans had been in abeyance to extend the Piccadilly Line both northwards and westwards. In 1932-3 much of the District Line from Hammersmith was widened to allow four-track running, and the Piccadilly was then extended in stages to Hounslow West over the route of the District. From Ealing Common to Uxbridge it took over the whole of the District route. The reconstruction of most of the stations here will be discussed more fully later, for they belong to the next phase of Holden's Underground station development. However, two of them fit into our current concern with development of the 'Morden' style. These were the new stations at Ealing Common and Hounslow West, completed early in 1931.

These two stations are very alike. Each has a polygonal booking hall set into a long single-storey building. The top of the hall stands proud and is decorated with the usual blue panels carrying information. In elevation the outside of Hounslow West has two layers, the base being of a grey granite effect with the rest in Portland stone. The booking hall at Ealing Common has lights on the ceiling, and an interwoven grey tile pattern around the edge. Hounslow West also has a tile pattern, made up of red and biscuit tiles, but features the original chandelier. This is unlike the exposed chandelier at Morden, for it echoes the design of the hall. Each of the seven light fittings has seven sides, and above this the ceiling features complex geometrical ribbing. Access to the offices and telephones is around the edge of the hall, and in the centre is a standard wooden ticket booth. This was the last real development of the style pioneered on the Morden line. New suburban stations would in future be built with a different approach.

The Operating Manager's Personal Letter detailing new projects, dated 30 March 1931, talks about the stations at Ealing Common and Hounslow West, and mentions the initiation of other new station buildings:

I cannot here say definitely what turn the architectural features of the new stations will take. Our architects have visited Continental buildings to absorb new ideas, not only in design but in types of material and methods of execution. Sudbury Town is now being erected as a specimen structure in the new programme. We want the stations to be original and approach the nearest to the ideal that may be practicable.

These tentative remarks belittle the innovations the Underground was about to make. The next developments will be detailed later.

It has been mentioned that the incorporation of the Metropolitan into what had been the Underground Group did not take place until 1933. When we left the Metropolitan some time ago it was undergoing a transformation into a modern electric railway, with new stations in town by C.W. Clark. The activities of the Metropolitan before it lost its independence must now be considered before the main story can be resumed.

It will be recalled that the Metropolitan had main line ambitions, and from 1906 the line northwards from Harrow-on-the-Hill was under joint control of the Metropolitan and Great Central (later the London & North Eastern Railway). Running arrangements were lax compared with the tight schedules of the Underground, and the Metropolitan's interest began to wander back closer to town. Instead of adding more branches at its extremes, two short spurs were added to attract new commuter traffic. The first of these was opened by the Metropolitan and LNER joint committee in 1925, from Moor Park (& Sandy Lodge) to Watford. The second was added in 1932 from Wembley Park to Stanmore and was entirely a Metropolitan effort.

The Watford line was originally intended to have three new stations, the two now in use (Croxley and Watford) and another in the centre of Watford. The first two were built in a simple domestic style unlike anything the Metropolitan had tried before. This is not to say that it was radical – far from it. Both Croxley and Watford were two-storey buildings, the upper storey projecting out through the sharply pitched roof. A greater contrast with the activity on the Morden line it is hard to imagine, but although not so important in terms of design, they are certainly well adapted to the new 1920s housing developments that sprang up around them.

Booking hall at Hounslow West The stock wooden ticket booth stands below a fascinating chandelier. Hounslow West and Ealing Common both featured individual tile designs and colour schemes in their booking halls

They are similar to Heaps' stations on the Edgware line in this respect, for they are unspectacular but not unpleasant. Unlike stations built by the Underground Group they do have some more outmoded features. The cumbersome canopies that jut out in front from the brick and slate cannot be free-standing but require inelegant iron pillars to support them. Another giveaway is that the buildings were heated by open fires – Croxley has four chimney stacks. Watford, although the terminus, was the smaller of the two stations, but this is explained by the fact that it was not intended to assume this role.

The third station on the line was to have been in Watford High Street, a logical site for a terminus. The plan was for the line to clip the edge of Cassiobury Park to the west of the town centre, and continue on to the High Street. When the company failed in purchasing land for the permanent way the scheme was abandoned, and Watford station was left as an unlikely terminus on the edge of Cassiobury Park – not even on a main road. However, the High Street station was completed before the Metropolitan realized it could not build a line to it! This station differed from the other two. It had a flat façade with decoration in Clark's white stone, which took up the ground floor. The second floor was faced in brick, with four windows with stone surrounds. The top of the building was fussily ornamented with architraves and carved faces. It would have been a fine terminal station, but the Metropolitan reluctantly had to sell it off. It opened up as a restaurant but was later taken over for use as the Grange furniture store.

Like the stations on the Watford line, those on the Stanmore branch were opened in what was then open countryside. Kingsbury, Canons Park and Stanmore were opened with the line in 1932, but Queensbury was not added until 1934. The design of the stations followed the Watford pattern, for they were also intended to fit in with the developing commuter areas. Kingsbury station had a central booking hall that stood taller than the rest of the building, which flanked it on either side. These portions were used as shops as a busy shopping street built up around the station building, which when erected had been totally isolated. The station really pretends to be a house, or perhaps a country cottage, and the deception is heightened by the false upper storey on the booking hall. When inside one can see that the hall

Croxley Similar to Watford, which was also opened in 1925, this station demonstrates the difference in approach by the Metropolitan and the Underground Group

Kingsbury Another branch station opened by the Metropolitan to generate new commuter traffic

continues almost up to the level of the roof.

The later station, at Queensbury, is less interesting, for it is built into one of those typical 1930s parades of shops that sprang up everywhere. Further north is a smaller version of this at Canons Park, but when one reaches the terminus at Stanmore the domestic style reasserts itself. There is more control exercised outside the building, for example, in the lighter canopy and supports superseding those at Croxley and Watford. Whereas buses and taxis had only a small forecourt at these two stations, a complete slip-road was provided at Stanmore to set it well back from the main road. Modifications since it was built have included more recent renovation in the ticket hall (down behind the main building, at platform level), and the buildings on the island platform.

Other stations in domestic style were also built before the Metropolitan lost its independence. The 1894 Wembley Park was enlarged in 1923 to cope with traffic for the British Empire Exhibition and the new 'Wembley' Stadium nearby. Further work was carried out in 1931, and the station was to reach its present form after more modifications in 1948. These last alterations were to provide a direct link with the stadium, but the main building is largely untouched – the booking hall retains the small green mosaic-like tiles used by the Metropolitan for decoration at the time, and the outside still carries the 1923 MR logo. The old Preston Road halt, which had been in use since 1908, was rebuilt in the same style as its contemporaries in 1931-2, with dark bricks and including a parade of shops.

The last station in effect to be built by the Metropolitan Railway was opened in November 1933, four months after the company had been absorbed into the new London Passenger Transport Board. It stood on a site not previously occupied by a station, between Pinner and Northwood, and was named Northwood Hills. Habitual travellers there will know that this station,

Stanmore Opened by the Metropolitan in 1932, this station formed a terminus for the Bakerloo from 1939 and the Jubilee from 1979

like the others, is now surrounded by a busy shopping street, but when it was opened it filled a gap in Metro-land that had not then been exploited. It was probably the simplest of the Metropolitan's new commuter stations – a bungalow building which contained just a booking hall and two shops – and is arguably the best of its type. Strangely enough, Pick and Holden were working on something entirely different, but before we rejoin them I should like to draw attention to the beginnings of a new spirit elsewhere on the system.

The most progressive of the main line companies was the Southern Railway, and one of its first major reconstructions involved the 1929 works at the old London & South Western station used by the District at Wimbledon, which it had recently acquired. Two entrances were constructed, one being larger than the other, with a forecourt and a hefty canopy over the entrances. The elevations were in white stone, similar to what Holden had been doing for the Underground group, and must have proved astonishingly different from the previous station. The imposing front of the main entrance is almost simpler than Holden's façades, except for the five large windows immediately above the entrance openings. Instead of emphasizing the vertical aspects with the glazing bars, as Holden had done, or even the horizontal, as might have been more expected, the fussy windows disturb the simplicity of Wimbledon station. A pattern of small interlocking arches was selected, with all the panes having to be cut to fit the awkward shapes that resulted. From a distance the windows therefore look as if they are hung with giant-sized net curtains, with only four vertical holes to each window. The Southern Railway was to rebuild many of its main stations in Portland stone with an art deco feel throughout the 1930s, though the only one that directly concerned the Underground was to be Richmond, also on the District, in 1937-8. There was a general trend in Britain towards modern railway architecture, but its high point was to be seen in the early 1930s as Charles Holden's Underground stations became some of the most important architectural innovators of the twentieth century.

4 The 'Classic Years' and Beyond

Early in 1931 a report was printed for private circulation entitled *A NOTE ON CONTEMPORARY ARCHITECTURE IN NORTHERN EUROPE (written as the result of a tour of Holland, Germany, Denmark, and Sweden made by Mr. Frank Pick, Mr. Charles Holden and Mr. W.P.N. Edwards 20 June–7 July 1930)*. The title is self-explanatory but does not reveal the reason for the tour. It was undertaken to find some inspiration for a radically new style of architectural design in accordance with Pick's desire to maintain the progressive image of the Underground and the rest of London's transport. The Group had had control for some time now of the major 'combine' omnibus companies, and with the possibility of the London Passenger Transport Act responsibility would be assumed for the remaining independent bus companies, along with all the tramways and the Metropolitan Railway. The situation excited Pick, for it would then be possible to coordinate the transport systems more effectively, as one organization. With the variations on the 'Morden' theme almost exhausted, he had asked Holden along on this jaunt to search for a new approach in keeping with his own forward-looking approach to design.

The results of the tour were rather patchy, for the party found that initiatives adopted varied widely from place to place. They found little to excite them in Germany and Sweden, and in Denmark it was a flair for total design of buildings and interiors that impressed most – even though the style of building did not merit pursuance. In Amsterdam, however, things began to jell, and working men's flats and the head office of the Tramways were impressive enough to be included in the report. Mention was also made of Bussum station. Throughout the Netherlands it was the use of a natural advantage – the red Dutch brick – which attracted most attention, particularly when used by Dudok in Hilversum. His thatched roof school was seen, and the party observed his town hall being built, admiring the Dutch civic sense. Dudok used brick in a way not generally seen, for his buildings showed that it was not just more attractive than plain stone or concrete, but could also be just as functional – there were no ornamental or neo-Georgian touches here – and the Dutch buildings had a national character, unlike the 'international' style found elsewhere. The report noted: 'Much of the work has been carried out by the architect Dudok, and great credit is due to him for the straightforwardness and vision of his work.' Holden now had his inspiration, and the party returned to London to begin work on new stations.

Similar to this new style were the Underground's buildings in Berlin, designed in 1929 by Grenander and opened in 1931. This was not on the itinerary, so Holden never saw what was then the most up-to-date collection of transport buildings in the world. Grenander's were, however, typically German, and lacked the sensitivity which Holden was to employ. It did not really matter in the long run, for the prototype station, at Sudbury Town, was ready for opening by July 1931.

The station at Sudbury Town had been chosen for the initial experiment, for the Piccadilly Line was due to take over running the stretch worked by the District, of which the old station formed a part. It was ideally situated away from main roads, so the work was carried out away from the public gaze. The result was a station with two entrances, one on either side of the tracks, joined by a covered concrete footbridge. The main entrance resembled that of Morden in shape – a large box in the middle with wings at either side. With the new use of load-bearing brick for the main structure, a concrete roof (in this case cast *in situ*) and stock metal-framed industrial windows, Holden found that he had a kit of parts with which to create related buildings for the other stations. Sudbury Town

SUDBURY TOWN

Main entrance Holden's brick-and-concrete solution to the problem of establishing a new architectural style. Sudbury Town influenced the design of Underground stations throughout the 1930s, and is now a listed building

Sudbury Town was the first of a new generation of stations that were to receive wide critical acclaim. Its appearance was that of a typical prototype, and several features differed from the stations that followed. Although let down by the standard of fitments, it established the general pattern for many other stations. Problems that arose here were resolved in the building of subsequent stations at Alperton and Sudbury Hill, but the major feature of the design survived intact – the load-bearing brick box with a flat concrete roof.

The roof at Sudbury Town was the only one to be cast in position as one piece, a procedure subsequently regarded as too awkward. The two vertical windows terminated short of the ground to form the entrances, whereas later stations had massive concrete beams or canopies above the openings. Though the buildings themselves were radical the layout of the station was not, following the Victorian pattern which retained the main construction alongside the tracks, with the southern platform linked to it by a footbridge. This bridge was of concrete, with a concrete roof, and could be used by ordinary pedestrians who wanted to cross the tracks as a matter of course. A small second entrance was constructed on the southern side.

Among the items retained was the wooden main ticket booth, of a design that had first appeared during the First World War. There was provision in the main building for a café. An experimental feature was the use of an illuminated station name on the cornice, which has since been removed.

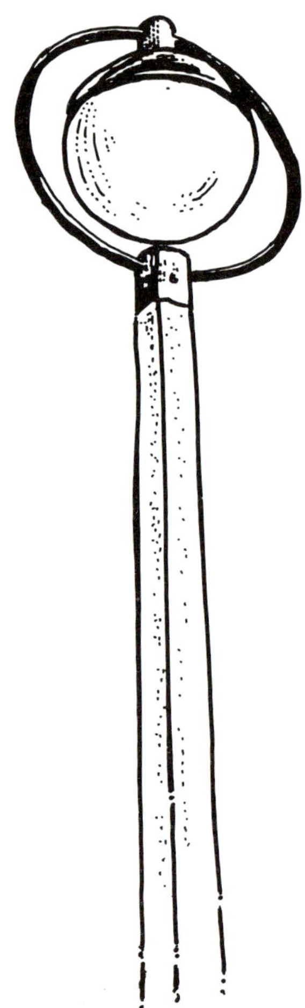

Lamp Although not responsible for interior fitments, Holden was able to design several ancillary items that were to recur at later stations, such as this simple lamp

Second entrance At stations with the main entrance alongside the tracks it is often convenient to construct extra access provisions for passengers approaching from the far side. This modest construction is stylistically related to the main building

Platform The platform canopies extend only the length of the station buildings and cover round-ended shelters for passengers. The absence of doors means that these cannot be regarded as waiting 'rooms'

Platform and concrete fence This view, from the footbridge, shows the open platform with flowerbeds, and Holden's solid precast concrete fence around the edge. This is the westbound platform, looking back towards Alperton

Sudbury Hill This was the second of Holden's Sudbury boxes, and avoided the minor problems that had arisen at Sudbury Town. The general design is much stronger here

was not a perfect station, but it showed the way ahead. It has earned both a listing by the Department of the Environment and the high praise of Sir Nikolaus Pevsner, who described it as a landmark heralding the 'classic phase of Underground architecture; 1930-1935 can be considered the "classic years"'.

Now that the idea had been established two further stations were opened, showing how the design could be adapted to different sites. Work was in progress on the replacement stations at Sudbury Hill and Alperton before Sudbury Town was completed. At Alperton the railway crossed the road on a viaduct, and the entrance was set back from the road to form a forecourt. A large building with two windows (similar, but in different proportions to Sudbury Town) was placed alongside the embankment, and the style was to be echoed on the other side of the railway where a large bus garage was built.

The site at Sudbury Hill was adjacent to the road bridge, beneath which was a cutting containing the railway. The station that Holden designed for this site was probably as much of a 'landmark' as Sudbury Town, for the architectural problems here resolved themselves to a sufficient extent for several later stations to be built in a similar manner. Unlike Sudbury Town or Alperton, here the entrance was stepped out from the main structure, and covered by a concrete canopy. There were large single windows on three sides of the 'box', and the separate letters forming the name of the station were placed on the concrete band on the extended portion, rather than high up on the band below the roof as at the other two. Brick and concrete were used throughout, and the station epitomizes Holden's declared aim of creating a 'concrete lid on a brick box'.

The next station was the important junction at Acton Town, where Piccadilly or District trains from Uxbridge, Hounslow and Ealing Broadway would all meet, requiring a cross-platform interchange. It was planned that, with quadrupling of the line from Northfields to the existing four tracks coming out of Hammersmith, Piccadilly trains should run non-stop from Acton Town to Hammersmith on the centre tracks with the District occupying the outer ones. To serve

Acton Town Another variation on the 'box' theme, adapted to a corner site with an extended lower portion. The station stands at an important junction of the Piccadilly and District Lines

the four tracks two island platforms were built, covered by concrete canopies with angled slab-like concrete supports painted grey below the centreline. A series of concrete bridges led up to the large booking hall, which had a main entrance in Gunnersbury Lane and a side entrance in Bollo Lane. The front was stepped out as at Sudbury Hill but on a grander scale, this lower section being extended towards the road junction.

Five more stations were directly affected by the multi-tracking of this route. At Hammersmith new platforms were built to the same pattern and style as Acton Town. Ravenscourt Park and Turnham Green already had old island platforms serving four tracks, so the District could be catered for here, but at Stamford Brook only the two southernmost tracks were served. Holden designed a bold new concrete canopy and platform, raised above the embankment on the north side for the District, leaving the eastbound Piccadilly Line with no platform connection.

Chiswick Park was completely rebuilt and opened in 1933. Here there were no connections with the Piccadilly Line at all, just a new platform of the Stamford Brook design serving each of the outermost tracks. The canopies for these platforms are sculpted with gentle curves rather than harsh angles. They are constructed entirely of boardmarked concrete, faced with small panels composed of biscuit-coloured tiles and enamel roundels. Halfway along each was a seat protected from the biting wind with glass panels, full-sized waiting rooms not being suitable. Holden had used Buckinghamshire brick to face his station buildings in order to prevent any staining by brown brake dust thrown out from the trains. These concrete canopies, however, have now gained a brown-orange tint after many years of being covered by this dust.

The station building at Chiswick Park is on the south side of the embankment carrying the railway, and consists of a semi-circular drum of bricks and windows, with a solid brick tower. It was hoped that this would attract attention to the station, which is well away from the main road, but it ended up looking like a redundant chimney stack. Towers were to continue to prove a problem.

The end of the quadrupled line lay at Northfields, where two island platforms were built. The station building was opened at the end of 1932, and was externally similar to Sudbury Hill but set well back from the road. The design was carried out in association with Stanley Heaps, the staff architect; the station name, instead of being picked out in individual letters, was displayed on a blue panel set into the extended canopy. Between Acton Town and Northfields was South Ealing, where only a temporary wooden entrance (still in use) was provided. The platform design was altered from that of Acton Town, with round-ended waiting rooms which were later repeated elsewhere. These completely new stations – Sudbury Town, Sudbury Hill, Alperton, Acton Town, Northfields and Chiswick Park (as well as the adaptation of South Ealing, Stamford Brook and Hammersmith) – formed the first phase of the new style at the western end of the Piccadilly Line. Also dating from 1932-3, there are stations at the northern end that are

Chiswick Park The main feature of this 1933 variation of Holden's theme is the semi-circular drum of the booking hall, with a solid brick tower to attract attention

part of the same family. The Cockfosters extension provided a showcase for eight brand new stations for which Holden had full control over every detail.

Pick had been very pleased with Sudbury Town station from an architectural point of view, and some of the interior design features, such as Holden's free-standing lamps, had also impressed. The engineering aspects for such common features as vending machines, or the lights on the footbridge, had nevertheless made him angry. He saw that they were not in sympathy with the station, having been added as an afterthought. It was almost as if there was a conspiracy to 'break up and destroy the tidiness and spaciousness of this station'. He was highly critical of many things, such as the 'illuminated tombstones' used for formal notices in the booking hall. In August 1931 he issued what amounted to a directive to the engineers' department in order to avoid future works being 'botched, just as Sudbury Town had to be botched'. Every miscellaneous detail was in future to be fully considered before work could be approved, and so Holden's responsibility was extended to cover redesign of many stock components. All his stations after Sudbury Town abandoned the wooden ticket booth for a redesigned metal-framed one, for which the bottom half was covered in simulated marble. Other items were also designed by Holden. These included subway entrances, light fittings, platform seats, clocks, kiosks, ticket machines, and even the five-feet tall concrete posts that held the cables at the side of the tracks. In the second half of the 1930s this work was also helped by Christian Barman, who would be Pick's biographer.

The Great Northern Railway's agreement with the original Piccadilly railway had forbidden any extension of the line north of Finsbury Park, and its successor, the London & North Eastern, went before a select committee of the Lords in May 1930 to prevent the proposed Cockfosters extension being built. Eventually Pick won the day, and set about planning what he believed would prove a model, setting new urban transport standards. The station sites almost suggested themselves at points where bus routes converged, and Holden delivered a varied selection of station buildings that justly complemented Pick's ideal.

The new line was opened to Arnos Grove on 19 September 1932, and included new stations at Manor House, Turnpike Lane, Wood Green and Bounds Green. The first of these had a sub-surface booking hall, like the stations in the centre of London, but with a low brick and concrete subway entrance. The station originally had a tram terminus, long since gone. At Turnpike Lane Pick found evidence that his instructions had been followed to the letter and he regarded the station as a total success. The Sudbury box was expanded and two large ventilation towers with louvred ports were added. Because the station stood on a corner site it was possible to construct a slip-road behind it to form a bus and tram station. The Underground roundel on the wall above the extended shop is not original, for when the station was opened the corner of the road was occupied by a very eye-catching feature – a reinforced concrete pillar with a circular flat canopy, above which was the staff and three-dimensional roundel found at other stations. At the top was a round metal skeleton supporting four lights. Although this has now gone, a similar construction (forming a pedestrian shelter) is still in place just to the north of Southgate station, and is listed for preservation separately from that station's main building.

The station at Wood Green consists of a semi-circular drum flanked by squared-off brick sections, and Bounds Green has a Sudbury box with chopped-off corners and a ventilation tower, but another listed building can be found at Arnos Grove. Here the line ran below the level of the road in a cutting, as at Sudbury Hill, and the building Holden designed was similar except that the booking hall was turned into a complete drum. It is a powerful sight which involved much complicated engineering, for after Sudbury Town was built no roofs were cast *in situ*. The front of the hall is surrounded by a symmetrically planed, flat-faced office building, in the middle of which is the entrance. As it was an open-air station the platforms were variations on the Acton Town pattern. At other stations on this extension with tube platforms a plain facing of biscuit-coloured tiles was used, with a narrow coloured band which varied between locations. The only other decoration was in the perforated art deco ventilation panels designed by Harold Stabler. One innovation at each of the new deep-level stations was an anti-suicide pit between the tracks to foil any would-be suicides. All other Tube stations below ground subsequently had these installed.

The widely admired Southgate station was opened in March 1933, at the same time as Enfield West (now Oakwood), which has also acquired a listed status. For the first time a station was designed with another outside architect, C.H. James, for Holden was increasingly under pressure from other commissions originating outside the Group. Enfield West followed the Sudbury Hill pattern of a box with an extended entrance, but on a grander scale. The terminus at Cockfosters was opened on 31 July 1933, at the end of the month that had seen the creation of the London Passenger Transport Board. Outside, the station had only two low brick subway entrances in the Manor House mould, but inside the concealed booking hall Holden had grasped the opportunity to make functional arrangements aesthetically pleasing. Angled concrete frames and pillars, developed from Acton Town, stretched down the platforms in the

Turnpike Lane Pick was particularly pleased with this combined bus and rail station, which was opened in September 1932 on the Arnos Grove extension

SOUTHGATE

Exterior The station is partly encircled by a matching brick building, separated by the slip road for buses

Southgate station is a unique example of the work of Charles Holden and remains today in almost exactly the same state as it was when opened in March 1933. The Piccadilly Line runs below in a short length of tunnel between neighbouring stations with open platforms (Arnos Grove and Oakwood).

The station is now a listed building, which accounts for the excellent state of preservation and retention of original details such as the lights mounted on pillars in the escalator shaft. These and other original examples of Holden's innovation have since disappeared from other contemporary stations. Southgate

Booking hall The ticket booth itself envelopes the base of the central column. Below its window level are panels of simulated marble, a feature which Holden used in other stations. In the background is the top of the escalator shaft

Escalator shaft This contains a flight of stairs flanked by two escalators in original condition. Illumination is provided by reflected light from the ceiling, the lamps being mounted between the escalator stairwells. In other stations these have now been removed and replaced by strip lighting. Bronze, brass and wood all combine to give a real feeling of quality

Standing lamp Two of these lamps stand at the foot of the escalator shaft, in a small hall between the platforms. Similar to, but larger than the escalator lamps, they also illuminate indirectly. The inverted white conical form at the top acts as a reflector for concealed lighting in the bowl

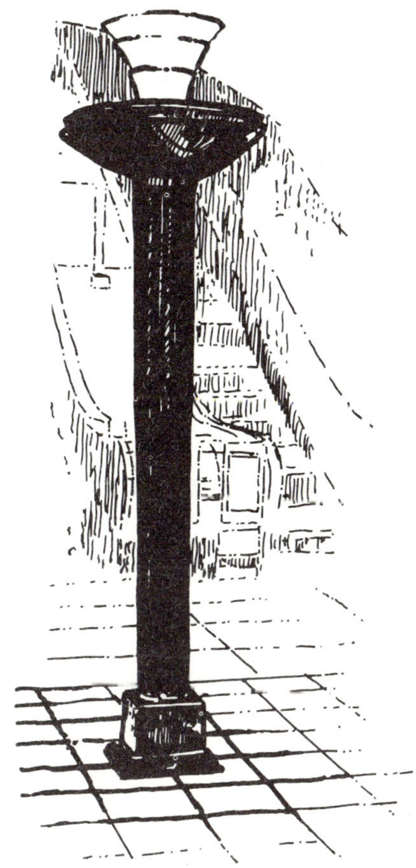

from the inside is a reminder of how they once looked.

From the outside, despite being obviously related to other 1930s stations, Southgate is strikingly individual. The estate agent's department had managed to purchase a large corner site, which Holden cut across with a private roadway with access for buses. Behind this he wrapped a solid brick façade, cut away at the bottom to provide space for shops and a waiting room. This formed a perfect backdrop to the station building itself, which he situated on the island formed at the tip of the corner. The overall appearance of this is of a glass drum surrounded by shops with an outer glass skin. There are flat roofs on two different levels, the central supporting column piercing through and continuing into an abstracted centrepiece crowning the building.

The success of the scheme led to Pick requesting the purchase of similar sites wherever possible.

Southbound platform Practically the only concession to more recent times is the fluorescent strip lighting along the ceiling. The walls are faced with the square biscuit-coloured tiles with black skirting. Between these is a narrow band of coloured tiles (yellow in this case) which is continued around the arches. The platforms are laid with conventional paving slabs

form of a nave and aisles. Apart from the geometric clarity of the arrangement the lighting from the windows was also reminiscent of a cathedral, while direct sunlight fell on to the posters exposed beyond the platforms. Routes containing various amenities fanned out from a central space, and Holden was sufficiently pleased with the interior of this station to adapt it later for the western terminus of the Piccadilly and Metropolitan Lines at Uxbridge.

The extension drew much attention when it was opened, and a supplement to the *Railway Gazette* was particularly pleased with the covered platforms provided for easy interchange with the trams at street level at Manor House and Turnpike Lane. The same article also noted that:

In those old stations which have been reconstructed on more attractive lines with additional entrances, and with escalators instead of lifts, it has been found that an immediate increase of some 20% in the number of passengers using them has taken place and has been sustained. This in itself is sufficient justification of the expense involved in the reconstruction or remodelling of the existing stations, and in providing what might to the uninitiated seem unduly lavish accommodation in the new ones.

The practical, inexpensive upkeep of high-quality materials such as polished hardwood and bronze were acknowledged, these advantages also including the appeal of the materials themselves. The article continued:

Bronze is usually associated with decorative finishings in consonance with its own artistic charm, and the use of this material for the very carefully designed handrails accentuates the crudity of certain untreated concrete walls, and creates an effect as incongruous as that of a beautiful woman in a drill hall.

Reflected lighting from wood and bronze stands provided illumination in booking halls and the escalator shafts, though most of the lamps have since been replaced by modern fluorescent lighting. Habitual passengers may be surprised to learn that the only stations which still have the upturned lamp standards between their escalators are Southgate and St John's Wood, whereas once they were to be found throughout London (having been installed with modern escalators at many stations between the late 1920s and the Second World War). The overall effect of Holden's décor was akin not so much to that of a luxury hotel as to the precision of the engine room of an ocean liner. Original black and white illuminated 'Way Out' signs and destination boards may still be seen in many revamped stations.

The significance of Southgate was revealed in an article in the house magazine *Pennyfare* in February 1934, which said:

With the district south-west of Arnos Grove already built up, and a lunatic asylum, sewage beds, and a cemetery in the area, development of a high class is handicapped. [However . . .] Southgate

Arnos Grove Now a listed building, Arnos Grove employs open platforms and this striking 'drum' booking hall, a logical development of the original Sudbury boxes

Boston Manor This station displays an attempt to break away from the monumentality of the Sudbury box by employing a tower as the chief eye-catching device

Osterley Dating from 1934 this station, like Boston Manor, uses a thin tower based on Dutch models that Holden had seen on the European visit in 1930

Rayners Lane Although supervised by Holden, this station was designed by R.H. Uren in a return to developments of the Sudbury box theme

station is similarly placed to Hendon Central, with a circus of 260 feet diameter focusing a number of main traffic thoroughfares. The traffic is beginning to grow, and 750 houses are included in the programme to mid-summer for the district. It is expected that Southgate will become one of the most important stations on the extension.

After the successful adaptation of his new style on the Cockfosters extension two new rebuilt stations, at Boston Manor and Osterley, were opened in 1934 on the Hounslow line. Whereas Holden had previously designed quite tall, solid buildings for stations, these two exhibit a different approach. The main part is a low single-storey building, but to attract attention a tower was added at each. These were different from the Chiswick Park or Turnpike Lane towers, for Holden had picked up on the 'thin towers' which he had seen in Holland during the European visit. Consequently these two stations were the closest that Holden came to the Dutch style, the towers having been inspired by others such as that by J.F. Staal on top of the Amsterdam *Telegraaf* newspaper building. The tower at Boston Manor took the form of an elegant 'slab' of bricks which was extended upwards with panels of translucent glass to a peak on one side that could light up at night. The Osterley tower was a very thin, multi-faceted obelisk atop a tall, square, brick pedestal. It was necessary because although the station was on a main road, the Great West Road, it was screened by the housing developments that took place on either side at about the same time. The next station to be completed was South Harrow in 1935. The building was here stepped up towards the railway which ran above, and one side was adapted to form a slip-road for use as a bus terminus.

The following year new buildings were opened at Park Royal. Although this station had been moved from the original District site in 1931 it was not actually reconstructed until 1936, when a new building with a rounded booking hall was opened. It was rather like Chiswick Park on a smaller scale and also had a square brick tower. It stood alongside the Western Avenue, and formed one end of a semi-circular parade of shops that curved away from the road. With its completion, the Piccadilly Line to South Harrow from Hammersmith now served only reconstructed stations, with the exception of North Ealing, still the only original Metropolitan District station on this stretch to remain.

It had been decided to renew some of the remaining stations of the Uxbridge line now that the Metropolitan, which owned the line from Rayners Lane to Uxbridge, was under the control of the rest of the Underground. In June 1938 the first of these, a stepped station similar to South Harrow, was opened at Ruislip Manor. In August it was joined by Rayners Lane, and by Uxbridge in December. The new building at Eastcote was added in 1939.

Rayners Lane was designed mainly by Reginald H. Uren, as Holden was still snowed under with other work. It was remarkable in differing from the Sudbury box by virtue of its unconventional position. Earlier stations had been set back from the general building line, and had been prominent because of their size and the height of the masts bearing the Underground roundel. Rayners Lane does not conform to this idea, for it literally 'sticks out'. The road runs over the tracks at a right-angle, and the usual solution would have been a Sudbury Hill type of station. The station would actually be built in conjunction with a new two-storey parade of shops on either side, so the opportunity was taken to pull the station out, or rather push the shops back, so that the booking hall would occupy the pavement. Entrances could therefore be provided at either side, instead of frontally, in line with the progress of pedestrians approaching it. The front line of kiosks stood proud of the general building line by some 25 feet, giving the station the importance it deserved at the connection of the Piccadilly and Metropolitan Railways. There is absolutely no chance of a passer-by not noticing this station. The rounded kiosks at the front of the building were retained at Eastcote, though this station otherwise reverted to the standard Sudbury Hill format in being set back from the building's extremities.

Mention was made earlier of the cathedral-like qualities of Cockfosters. If the great vaulted roof main line stations could be described as the nineteenth century equivalent of the great medieval churches, then it was certainly a tradition continued on a smaller scale in the 1930s by Holden and his team. When the Uxbridge terminal station, on a new site, was opened in December 1938 it formed the logical development from Cockfosters. A large surface building with direct access to the platforms was provided, so a passenger had no stairs to negotiate. Above the booking hall there was even a stained-glass window, the only one of its kind on the Underground. The station was designed with L.H. Bucknell, and it virtually concluded work on the Piccadilly Line.

Holden's involvement with the Underground was not yet over, as he was also working, along with Heaps and others, on designs for improvements and extensions on the Central, Bakerloo and Northern Lines, the last of which had only recently lost its cumbersome title of 'Edgware, Highgate and Morden Line'. This was in association with the 1935-40 New Works Programme, which was to be interrupted by the war and never fully completed. But before we go on to this subject more fully it would be wise to return to the rebuilding programmes of the main line companies as they affected the Underground.

Many of the Underground stations are today still administered by

Diagram of Rayners Lane When completed in 1938 this station was unique in having a booking hall stepped out from the line of shops, built at the same time to emphasize the main building

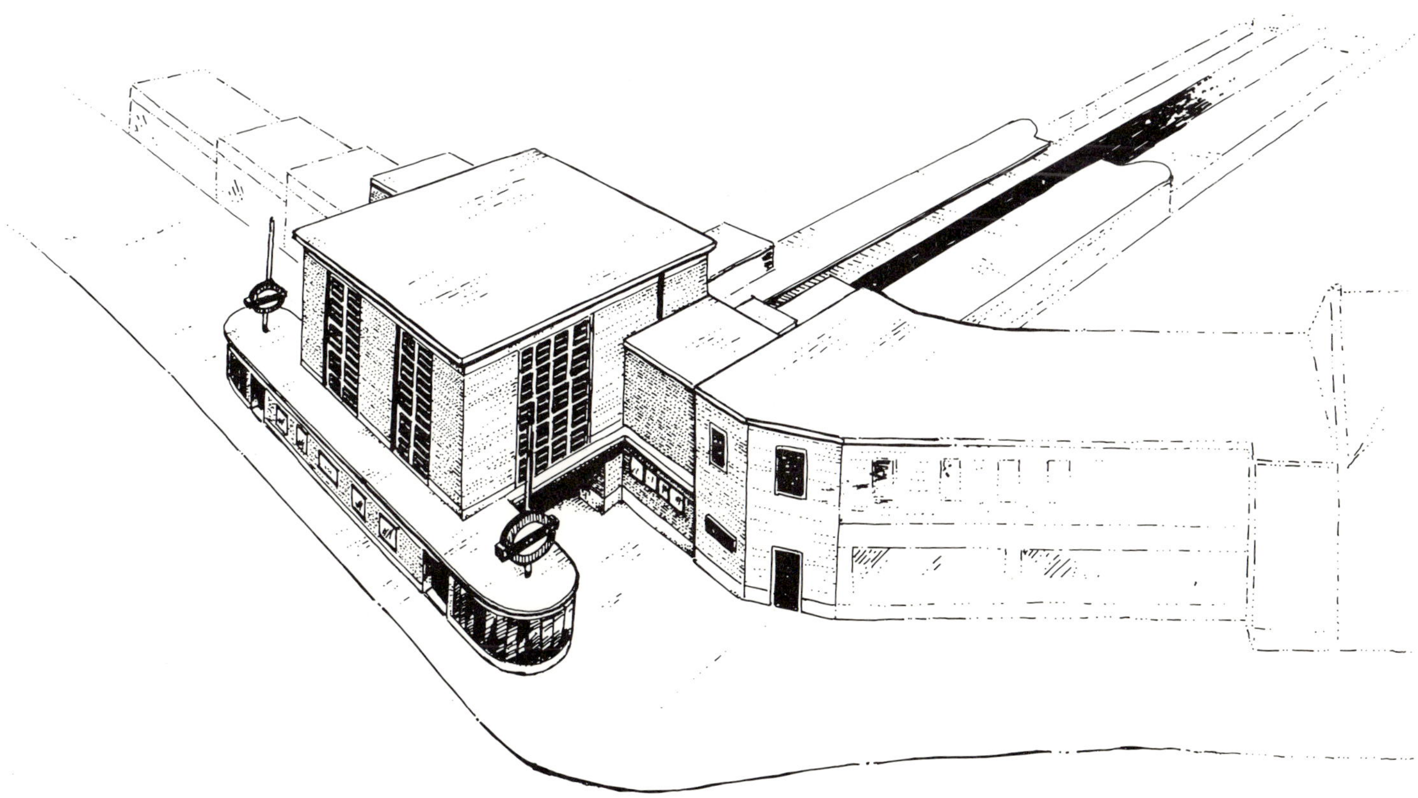

UXBRIDGE

General view The station stands near the High Street, the entrance façade derived from the building that stands behind the booking hall at Southgate. With the entrance in the centre, the two wings are provided with shops at ground floor level

Designed in collaboration with L.H. Bucknell, the terminus at Uxbridge was opened at the end of 1938 when the previous terminal station in Belmont Road was closed. It was the end of both the Metropolitan and the Piccadilly Lines, and was a development of Holden's earlier Piccadilly terminus at Cockfosters. The platform design was similar, as was the main circulating area, and there was a side access from the bus station. This complemented the main entrance, which formed part of a semi-circular frontage with a forecourt. This forecourt was originally adorned with overhead wires for turning round trolleybuses.

Instead of reflected lighting, the station was lit by suspended spherical lamps. The interior was largely undecorated, leaving the plain boardmarked concrete exposed. A café, toilets, shops and offices were also incorporated into the complex. There was little ornamentation, but twin concrete sculptures were placed above the main entrance and the station has the only stained-glass window on the Underground.

The treatment of Uxbridge and Cockfosters differs markedly from that of Edgware and Morden, built in the previous decade. Much of this can be attributed to technical improvements in materials, but equally important was the Pick–Holden desire to create totally modern stations. Like its contemporaries, Uxbridge has dated little and has recently earned listed building status.

Stained-glass window This unique feature emphasizes the cathedral-like effect of the architecture. It is placed over the passageway leading back to the main entrance

Entrance The concrete canopy is supported by two pillars. The twin sculptures placed symmetrically atop the building appear abstract, but are derived from upturned wheels and leaf springs

Platforms This shows one of the 'aisles' of the Uxbridge 'cathedral'. The canopy stops short of the side wall (which has panels of biscuit tiling). This wall and its advertisements are thus lit by direct sunlight

Interior view The modernity and spaciousness of Uxbridge was largely a result of this circulating area. To the left, before the platforms, is the exit to the bus station

Dagenham East This station building dates from 1932, and was built by the LMS in connection with an electrification scheme to allow District trains to run a through service to Upminster

British Rail. These involve stations on the District's Richmond line, the Wimbledon branch (south of the river), the line between Upminster and Barking, Ealing Broadway, and the Bakerloo from Queen's Park northwards. The Victoria Line also has main line associations. As we have noted before, companies such as the Southern Railway (amalgamated by nationalization in 1948) were carrying out their own modernization programmes in the 1930s.

The District railway to Upminster was the subject of a modernization schedule in the early 1930s at the same time as Holden was developing his new style. The London, Tilbury & Southend Railway had been taken over by the Midland Railway in 1912, and when that company was absorbed into the London, Midland & Scottish, it was decided to widen the Southend line between Barking and Upminster to four tracks to provide an added facility for local traffic. The District had operated this line from 1902 to 1905 when electrification had cut back the terminus to Barking, and the LMS agreed to electrify the new tracks to enable the District Line once again to finish at Upminster.

The old London, Tilbury & Southend stations as far as Barking (which had itself been enlarged in 1908) were largely undisturbed when the widened extension tracks were opened in September 1932. Only the track layout at Barking was altered, but the stations to Upminster took on a new appearance. First up the line was Upney, a completely new station. Next was Becontree, another new station built to replace Gale Street Halt, which had opened in 1926. A station was constructed at Heathway (now Dagenham Heathway), and Dagenham (East), Hornchurch and Upminster were all rebuilt. All these new stations were built roughly to the same design, featuring single-storey, dark brick buildings. Upminster was larger than the others, and the front has since been rebuilt with light grey bricks. The other stations are identical from the outside.

The LMS, like Holden, has chosen to keep clear of the stark, white façades of so much modern architecture, but it had also wanted to have an up-to-date approach. The cost of updating the line prohibited extravagant experimentation, and so the same simple, indistinguishable buildings were constructed at each one. The front elevation of each station consists of a low brick wall, stepped up twice towards the centre. The entrance is roughly central with large windows on either side in which the panes are divided up by almost square-patterned regular grids. Above the windows and entrance is a flat canopy with a plain white edge which is almost as long as the front of the building itself. Each station was built on the road above track level. The most interesting is probably Dagenham East. Three platforms were provided, one on either side of the through lines and a third for use as a terminal. This platform is particularly awkward to use for it is staggered some way down, and on the other side of, the main eastbound platform. A passenger can have been informed that the next train westwards is due to leave from the infamous platform 3, and be some way down towards it, before the train pulls out and the unlucky victim has to traipse all the way back to the main building and cross the line to the westbound platform. From here he may see a rarity on London's Underground, for this is part of an island platform fenced off down the middle. Beyond the barred section are the main line British Rail tracks with their overhead cables, followed by another platform and the original Dagenham station of 1885, which had been used by the District during its previous short-lived Upminster excursions between 1902 and 1905. Although it is no longer in use as a station, the old platform canopy remains, and the forecourt provides parking space for a garden centre.

The line was sufficiently popular for the LMS to build two further intermediate stations – at Upminster Bridge (1934) and Elm Park (1935). The Elm Park building resembled the earlier ones, and a long sloping gangway was provided down to platform level. Upminster Bridge provided a welcome relief from the other rather monotonous designs. The booking hall was below platform level, and although the façade was similar to the other buildings a high polygonal booking hall was provided. Possibly inspired by Holden's experiments, this was on a far less grand scale, but stood proud of the flat structure as Ealing Common or Hounslow West had done. The facing was in the same dark brick used at the other stations, and the hall was tiled within.

Reference has been made to the new stations of the Southern Railway. Its new station at Richmond (the south-western terminus of the District) was opened in 1937, although reconstruction was not fully completed until 1938. The company was remaining faithful to its plain masonry, but the station that resulted is far more solid and imposing than that of Wimbledon, built almost ten years previously. A slip-road was provided in the forecourt, and above the entrance were three large windows. The narrow, rectangular panes were set into dark-painted industrial metal frames similar to those used by Holden, with the centre one being partly occupied by a clock. There were two hefty flagpoles on either side of these main windows, attached to the wall at an angle. There are faint marks still visible high up on the front where the individual letters making up the words 'Southern Railway' once were.

The main construction work at Richmond did not affect all the platforms. Those used today by the District Line are probably the oldest in the station, with ornate ironwork from the original station still visible on the canopy supports.

Another station with a plain exterior which fits into this era is Wembley Central. There had been a station on this site since the London & Birmingham's Sudbury of about 1842, after which administration had passed to the London & North Western, which renamed it Sudbury & Wembley (1882) and

Upminster Bridge Built in 1934 between Hornchurch and Upminster, this station displays a more adventurous treatment using stock components by the LMS

Richmond The Southern Railway continued the use of white stone facing at its rebuilt stations; this one, used by the District, was completed in 1938

Wembley for Sudbury (1910), and the station was used from 1917 by the Bakerloo. The new design was typical of the 1930s but was only completed before nationalization, British Railways renaming the station 'Wembley Central' in July 1948. It was one of the few stations on the Bakerloo's Watford line which the LMS worked on during this period, although Carpenders Park was later rebuilt by BR in 1952.

The design of Wembley Central is different from many other suburban stations. With Wembley High Road likely to develop into a main shopping street, it was natural to want an elongated frontage with space that could be let to shops, but instead of having these on either side of the main entrance two separate entrances were provided at either end of the shopping 'block'. These two entrances connected up behind the shops in a long covered hall leading to the booking hall itself. The tracks run underneath the road at right-angles, but there is no sign of them from the main road as contemporary buildings run across the bridge on the other side. Decoration on the front of the station was confined to simple art deco projections between the two main upright windows over each entrance. Horizontal ridges link the windows over the shops, which are fitted with square panes in metal frames.

The Bakerloo Line is unusual in having shrunk so much in route mileage in recent years, with only a skeleton service (discontinued in 1982) operating beyond Queen's Park or Stonebridge Park to Watford Junction. In 1939 it took over the Metropolitan's Stanmore branch, only to relinquish it to the Jubilee Line forty years later. One might be forgiven for thinking that in the 1980s the cost-cutting contraction and rationalization of the Underground, which threatens a number of stations, is a modern phenomenon. This is not so, for under the Pick–Ashfield administration of the 1930s many similar ideas were advanced as Pick saw that the modern improvements to the system must be balanced by removal of obstacles which made it more difficult to operate. The first priority was to improve the efficiency of the Metropolitan. The joint committee that controlled the line north of Harrow was to be overhauled so London Transport would have permanent responsibility for the line as far as Amersham and the LNER would handle all stations beyond. Pick argued (in terms familiar to us today) that London Transport could not be expected to run a proper service at the Metropolitan's extremities, and the old company's outer limits were closed down. Services on the Brill Branch were ended in 1935, and the following year all stations on the Verney Junction line north of Aylesbury ceased to be served by Metropolitan trains (although Quainton Road was brought back into use temporarily from 1943 to 1948). When the Bakerloo was extended to Stanmore the Metropolitan ceased to work its stations between Neasden and West Hampstead. The tube also opened new stations at St John's Wood and Swiss Cottage, which were to replace three other Metropolitan stations: Lords/St John's Wood, Marlborough Road, and its own Swiss Cottage. Several old station sites had been closed when new replacements were opened, including a new Aldgate East, which had a very simple concrete entrance below which were new platforms which could accommodate two more cars per train. The old District Aldgate East and St Mary's were closed when this was opened in 1938.

In association with the modernization of the Piccadilly Line Pick proposed closing several stations that he thought were too close together (he was criticized over the wide spacing of the Cockfosters extension station when that was opened). He believed that the distances involved with unnecessary stations would slow trains down too much, but in the event he only succeeded in closing down three of the old Piccadilly stations: Down Street and York Road (1932) and Brompton Road (1934). A precedent had of course been set when the 'Northern' line works were under way in the 1920s, City Road closing in 1922 and South Kentish Town in 1924.

It will be obvious that the 1930s were a busy time for the Underground. The most important stations by Holden do not seem dated even today, mainly because he and Pick knew what their aims were; that is to say, what Pick said would ensure 'the establishment of goodwill and good understanding between the passengers and the company'. The station had to be an attractive shop to receive clients, and Holden's stations became galleries of graphic art with Pick's posters and innovations on display. Pick saw the entire exercise as an experiment in design education for the masses, and despite this anti-democratic view of giving the public what he thought it ought to have, rather than what it might have wanted, the new stations and designs were readily accepted. The design of many schools, colleges and other public buildings of the 1930s followed Holden's lead in the

Wembley Central This station was rebuilt with white facing by the LMS and was renamed 'Wembley Central' after nationalization in 1948

use of brick, concrete and stock metal windows. Any criticism of Holden's work is only possible because the best of it is so good, variety rather than uniformity having formed his station concept.

It is interesting that the most influential phase of Holden's work was inspired by the European tour. In September 1932 the Danish publication *Arkitekten* published a review of his work from the 1920s stretching over twenty-four pages. The article was comprehensively illustrated with photographs of stations, and Piccadilly Circus and 55 Broadway were discussed in detail. It was totally overwhelmed by these as it tried to set them in the context of good design and planning within London's streets. There was a comparison of approach, with photographs, posters and signs in Copenhagen to back up this argument. Holden had sought inspiration in Europe, and in Europe his flair for design was in turn recognized.

5 The New Works Programme and Post-War Developments

The Bakerloo was, as already mentioned, one of the first lines to show any benefit from the massive 1935-40 New Works Programme. In order to relieve pressure on the Baker Street to Wembley part of the Metropolitan, which at that time carried Metropolitan trains outwards to four (five including the Chesham branch) termini, that line was to bypass many of its old stations, which would henceforth be served by the Bakerloo on its way to Stanmore. The most congested part of the old Metropolitan route was the line between Baker Street and Finchley Road, so a new tube for the Bakerloo was built to bring the tracks to the surface at Finchley Road. Two new intermediate stations were opened, at St John's Wood and Swiss Cottage, for the Bakerloo in 1939.

The work on these two new stations was carried out by the staff architect, Stanley Heaps, in the style that Charles Holden had developed. While Holden had been busy with stations and other projects, Heaps had had to content himself with designing ancillary buildings and engine sheds, but with Holden's attention being increasingly diverted away from the Underground, Heaps was called in to cope with the Bakerloo's requirements. Although the two stations are similar below ground, St John's Wood is the more interesting because it also has surface buildings, built on steel frames. The booking hall is in the form of a drum, with a main clerestory window divided up by vertical concrete bars rather than the usual metal frames. The entrance fans out with a shop on either side covered by the flat canopy, and in front of it are small lawns surrounded by plants and low concrete walls. This is an interesting departure, for before this any extra space on a corner site such as this had been used purely for functional purposes, usually a slip-road or forecourt for

St John's Wood This is Heaps' successful attempt to work with the new style; the station building dates from 1939, but the storeys above are a later addition

EAST FINCHLEY

East Finchley was opened in 1939 for Underground trains on the site of a former Edgware, Highgate & London station. It was necessarily a large undertaking, designed to form a turnaround point requiring canteen and train crew facilities. Both Holden and L.H. Bucknell worked on the station, but its general appearance was less coherent than their earlier Uxbridge collaboration. It does, however, have some interesting features, which make it stand out as the last major Holden station of the 1930s.

The track is carried over the main road at an angle on a viaduct, and the massive main building is on the eastern side of the station. A second entrance, from the Causeway, is also provided, linked by a passage under the tracks to the booking hall. The platforms are therefore reached from beneath. They are also linked by a built-up footbridge for staff, with access from two spiral

Main entrance Directly above the main entrance is the figure of the Archer. Behind this can be seen the two enclosed spiral staircases that link the platforms to the footbridge and offices

Waiting room East Finchley was contemporary with the adaptation of old Metropolitan stations for the Bakerloo. The new platforms all featured these round-ended waiting rooms at the end of the platform buildings

Second entrance The second entrance, from the Causeway, is on the western side of the station and is stepped further out from the main structure. It takes the form of a polygonal box grafted on to the station

staircases built into the southern end of the platforms.

Eric Aumonier, who had provided a sculpture for 55 Broadway some ten years earlier, was commissioned to design another for one of the parapets on the eastern side. The powerful figure of the 'Archer', aiming in the direction of London, symbolizes the rapid transit of modern electric trains and is the most distinctive feature of the station.

Statue of Archer Aumonier's imposing sculpture is lead-encased, with a brass bow and details

Platforms The design of the platform buildings and canopies is derived from an experimental style pioneered at South Ealing. There are panels of biscuit tiles, and narrow tiled bands in black, yellow and turquoise

High Barnet The main station was built in 1872 by the Great Northern, and this booking hall, on the hill, was added in 1896. The LNER adapted the station in 1940 for the arrival of Underground trains

buses, and could be explained by a road-widening scheme which was under consideration at the time. Heaps was also keen to make his work attractive. Like others, this station was designed to be built upon, and it too has received upper storeys that are bland and unsympathetic to it.

The décor inside the booking hall resembles the sub-surface one at Swiss Cottage, with a reversion to wood rather than simulated marble around the ticket booths. False ceilings of asbestos cement board were used over escalator shafts and in St John's Wood booking hall, the latter laid out in a web pattern. The escalator lamps were originally of Holden's reflective designs, and are still in place at Swiss Cottage. Other interior lighting, however, was not by free-standing reflective lamps but by the suspended globes that Holden had taken to using later on, for example at Uxbridge. These remain at St John's Wood. At the foot of the escalators at each station was a concourse between the platforms, at the end of which were offices and fire-fighting equipment (buckets and hoses) behind glass-panelled bronze doors. The only real difference between the cream-tiled platforms at each station is in the colouring of the edging bands – brown and yellow at St John's Wood, brown and green at Swiss Cottage. St John's Wood also has random tiles with moulded pictures on them, including a portrait of Thomas Lord, after whom the nearby Lord's Cricket Ground is named. Both have station names displayed on tiled friezes at head height along the platforms.

Although the link between the Bakerloo and Metropolitan involved complicated civil engineering problems, only minor reconstruction was carried out at other affected stations. The Finchley Road platforms were altered, and the 1938 work at West Hampstead included redecoration of the booking hall and installation of a simulated marble ticket booth. The platforms were also rebuilt with round-ended concrete canopies and waiting rooms of the kind pioneered at South Ealing. This platform style was also applied to Kilburn and Dollis Hill, the latter having a new booking hall below the tracks reached from small brick entrances in Chapter Road and also on the other side of the line. At both Neasden and Willesden Green an old disused platform of the Metropolitan can still be seen on the south-western side of the tracks.

At about the same time as the transfer of the Stanmore branch to the Bakerloo, Harrow-on-the-Hill, which also carried LNER tracks, was reconstructed. The emphasis for a station entrance had shifted from the hill side to College Road, and the new brick-built station formed a bridge over the tracks containing the booking hall and ancillary offices, including a relay room and, at the top, a signal box. The idea of building the station as a bridge rather than a subway was to help reduce the moisture and dirt which would otherwise accumulate through gravity. Although reconstruction at Harrow-on-the-Hill was begun in 1939 it was not complete until 1948. The old station at Northwood was later to be rebuilt in a more modest fashion.

The Metropolitan was involved in a complex project at King's Cross to separate it from the old 'Widened Lines' and to link it to the Northern and Piccadilly. The two tubes were served by a new booking hall with standard cream décor from June 1939, and the new Metropolitan station was opened in March 1941. It involved a separate booking hall between the platforms, with a large extended concourse. This was a feature which was widely admired on the new Moscow Metro which had been opened only a few years before, and the architects' department had determined to incorporate the idea into some new stations.

The New Works Programme provided for further northward extensions of the Northern Line, from Edgware to Bushey Heath, and from Highgate (Archway) to High Barnet and Mill Hill East. The war interrupted progress and the extension from Edgware was never built, the Aldenham train depot provided for it later being converted into a bus overhaul works.

The High Barnet line opened in April 1940, although trains had been running to the new East Finchley station since the previous July. This station was designed by Holden with L.H. Bucknell, who had worked with him on Uxbridge station. It was the last of the major stations of the 1930s that Holden worked on, but it lacked the attractions of his previous work. Its best-known feature is actually Eric Aumonier's archer sculpture. North of East Finchley the Northern Line worked over London & North Eastern Railway tracks, and no major station rebuilding was ever carried out. Finchley Central is a very old station, originally opened in 1867 by the Edgware, Highgate & London Railway. The building has light-coloured bricks and there is an old footbridge across the line. The platform canopies are the old serrated edge type, now painted green. Travelling north the next station is West Finchley, which had been opened by the LNER in 1933, with small wooden platform buildings. Woodside Park, Totteridge & Whetstone and High Barnet were all built by the Great Northern Railway and date from 1872. They are also predominantly built of light brick, although the Totteridge building, on a bridge over the tracks, has more recently had a completely new roof added, with a front extension. It also has small brick platform buildings with serrated canopies.

The old station at High Barnet, which formed the northern terminus of the extension, is probably

Mill Hill East This is the terminal station of a branch of the Northern Line, built in 1867 by the Edgware, Highgate & London Railway

the most attractive. The main station building is on the western platform, but the booking hall is on a higher level back up towards the road. It is reached by a narrow footpath reminiscent of a country lane, which slopes steeply down from the road and continues down behind the main building and beyond. The booking hall peeps out from behind clumps of foliage, giving it a secluded image very different from other terminal stations on the Underground.

In January 1941 the reconstruction of Highgate (Archway) was completed and a new station, Highgate, was opened between here and East Finchley. The entrance to this station was from a car park built on the side of Highgate Hill, and passing into the passage one has to descend to platform level by escalators. The platforms are decorated with the station name being picked out in single letters on individual tiles running the length of the platform wall at head height, in the manner of St John's Wood and Swiss Cottage. The same technique was used at the Metropolitan's King's Cross station, opened the same year, and at other 1940s works, though it was afterwards standard practice to use enamelled metal signs to form this continuous band.

Four months after Highgate was completed the old Edgware, Highgate & London station at Mill Hill East was opened up to the Northern Line, reached by an old route which formed a spur from Finchley Central. The 1867 building remains largely in its original state, and up behind it is the single platform, as only one set of tracks now leads into the station. The platform is constructed of wooden boards and does not even have a canopy to protect passengers from bad weather.

The most ambitious plans of the New Works Programme involved the projected extensions to the Central Line. Frank Pick had long desired this work to be carried out, feeling that the middle portion of the Central was being under used. As with all the branch lines, the idea was to feed the main section with traffic to bring it up to proper working efficiency. The line was still working with its original (though modified) rolling stock, powered by the three-rail system installed in 1900. The new plan would mean converting all the line to the standard four-rail system, replacing the trains, and negotiating running powers over routes owned by the main line companies. It will be obvious that this had become a common technique, for since the early 1900s only the Edgware, Morden and Cockfosters extensions had not involved running over another line's route, Underground controlled or otherwise. In the east the Central Line would be extended to join the LNER at Stratford, where it could run northwards over a route originally opened by the Eastern Counties Railway in 1856. The line could continue to Ongar from Loughton on a Great Eastern Railway route of 1865. Also, by adding a new tube between Leytonstone and Newbury Park the Central could join that company's 1903 route in a loop back to Woodford. To the west it was planned for the Central Line to join the old Great Western & Great Central joint line at North Acton and to continue along it to Denham, though after the war the terminus was cut back to West Ruislip. This line had always been undersubscribed since it was built (from London to Birmingham) at the end of the nineteenth century, the last main line ever built into London, and the Great Western welcomed the chance of handing the commuter service over to London Transport.

Work on the Central Line began before the war, with the reconstruction of Liverpool Street into a combined station for the Central, Circle and Metropolitan Lines. Work was begun at other stations but was held up during the war, so the new line eastwards did not begin to accept trains until 1946. Pick never lived to see it, for he retired from the Board in 1940 after he found that he and Lord Ashfield no longer held the same policy views. The single post of chief executive was abolished and replaced by six new departmental heads, and without Pick to guide the fundamental strategy of design with a high standard of service London Transport

was left without a clear picture of the way ahead. Pick missed the driving force of his work and never adapted to life without it. He died of a brain haemorrhage on 7 November 1941, aged sixty-two.

With Pick gone, Holden finally drifted away from the Underground scene. Only three of the stations on the new Central Line extension were designed by him, and although design work had been carried out before the war the energetic spirit of the inter-war years had vanished. Besides Pick, the railways manager, the chief engineer and Heaps, the staff architect, were all lost to the Board. Ashfield remained until 1947.

The first stage of the Central Line extensions opened in December 1946 with a new station at Bethnal Green, a link with the District at Mile End, and a link with the LNER at Stratford. The Bethnal Green platforms had the station name in tiles in the manner of St John's Wood. Random tiles had relief pictures including St Paul's Cathedral, the LT roundel and 55 Broadway. The station was not lit by Holden's lamps on the escalators or elsewhere, for like all the post-war stations it was fitted out with the newly invented fluorescent lighting (described by Grahame Middleton as 'that great architectural killjoy'). The earliest holders to be used for these had a particularly awkward and cumbersome triangular cross-section. Mile End had a different platform layout, for a clever reconstruction had resulted in a cross-platform interchange below ground. The Central ran up close to the surface to appear on either side of the District tracks, with two island platforms separating them all. Outside, the station showed a reversion to the flat 'Morden' screen of the 1920s with the pale exterior being edged with a blue stripe, which although simple enough was rather a fussy decoration to apply to such a modern station.

Stratford station had undergone several reconstructions since it was first opened by the Eastern Counties Railway in 1839. For the arrival of the Underground the old main entrance was closed, and the south side of the station was rebuilt between 1939 and 1946. The platforms for LNER electric trains and the Central Line were completed in time for the opening of the tube service next to the old station.

Stratford This main entrance was rebuilt during the war by the LNER and was completed in 1946 for combined use by main line and Underground services

Snaresbrook Served by the Central Line since 1947, parts of the station date from the 1940s but the platforms from 1856. The main building was rebuilt by the Great Eastern in 1893

In order to use the station the running tunnels for the Central were sharply angled upwards, so the station became a 'hump' in the open that trains would run up to, diving down again at the far end. Constructions on the platform were in the form of slabs, faced in light-coloured matt tiles, and shops and a café were provided. The booking hall was beneath the platforms, reached by a subway that was given a grand entrance covered in the same tiling as the platforms in the form of large stepped blocks. At the base was the opening, which is today also connected with a modern link to a nearby shopping centre.

In May 1947 the Central Line reached its two next stations, at Leyton and Leytonstone. The old Eastern Counties station at the former on the west side was augmented by the present entrance on the bridge by the Great Eastern in about 1879. For the Underground it was redecorated with a new flat plaster front being added parallel with the road. There are still some original decorative iron canopy supports for the open platform canopies at the western end. The LNER reconstructed Leytonstone in 1946-7 with two small plain brick entrances leading to a booking hall beneath the tracks.

The fork for Woodford and Newbury Park opened in the following December. On the Woodford line the Central took over the old intermediate stations at Snaresbrook and South Woodford, with new stations on the Newbury Park line. Snaresbrook was an Eastern Counties station of 1856, although modifications were made to it during its long history which included a new booking hall and the addition of a bay platform on the western side in 1893. An additional entrance on the eastern side was provided by the Great Eastern in 1903, but with the arrival of the Underground this was replaced by a small plain brick booking office with restricted opening hours. This addition took place in October 1948 and the main station building was altered by grafting on a similar construction at the side to form the main booking hall. The platforms are largely unaltered serrated-valance canopied constructions with iron supports, but whereas the London-bound one is a standard side platform the other is an island platform with tracks only on one side. The bay it had also served was closed in 1950 and replaced by the station car park.

The station at South Woodford had also been one of the original Eastern Counties stations, but the present main building dates from its reconstruction by the Great Eastern in 1882-3. This building differs from the one at Snaresbrook as it is only a single-storey construction.

Wanstead One of Holden's last commissions, Wanstead was designed before the war but not opened until 1947. Its plain concrete facing marked another change in direction by the architect

There had been one of six level crossings on the line here but this was closed in November 1947 when the line was electrified. Like Snaresbrook, the station had an additional entrance on the other side of the tracks, opened in 1948. South Woodford had been known as George Lane for most of its life, but the former name has always been used since the Central Line extensions.

Woodford was reconstructed by the Great Eastern in 1888-92, similar to Snaresbrook in having a two-storey building (with most of the windows now bricked up). An extra entrance on the east side was opened as part of this scheme. Like most of the stations on this stretch of line, Woodford retains its old platforms, which are crossed by a footbridge.

The stations at Wanstead, Redbridge and Gants Hill were the last complete stations with which Charles Holden was commissioned. They had been designed before the war but completed afterwards, resulting in the original lighting being fluorescent and a great deal of work being carried out in timber, presumably because of the scarcity of bronze. Wanstead, the first station on the branch, has a rectangular booking hall with a longitudinal clerestory roof which makes the building look as though it has two floors. Passenger entrances are from the side, while at the western end is a large ventilation tower that stands over a circular shaft. The whole of the exterior proved a departure from Holden's use of brick, with a plain finish of grey cement. Inside, the station is decorated in the style of its contemporaries, with strip lighting and random relief cream tiles, though only with the LT roundel (which is coloured for the tiled platform nameband). The station platforms are given a colour coding of green in the form of a narrow stripe.

From Wanstead the trains continue in tube tunnels under the

South Woodford Formerly known as George Lane, this main building is an example of a Great Eastern reconstruction in 1882-3. The entrance on the other side of the tracks was added in 1948

Redbridge Opened at the same time as Wanstead and Gants Hill; these stations mark the end of Charles Holden's association with the Underground

Eastern Avenue to Redbridge and Gants Hill. Only Redbridge has a surface building, a circular booking hall which was described in the *Railway Gazette*'s publication *Improving London's Transport* in 1946 as '. . . consisting in plan of two concentric circles with the annulus between them symmetrically divided to give three entrances, two shops, two lavatories, a ticket office, and a tobacco kiosk . . . A tower built over the head of the escalator with supporting wings prevents the station from looking like an insignificant ventilating shaft, transformer kiosk, or pump house.' The station is almost like a mini Southgate with a square bit on the end, cut off from the corner by a slip-road used by buses. The roundel as a decorative feature peppers the inside of the station wherever one looks, so one cannot be in any doubt about who operates it. The platforms form an 'island' just below the surface, and were constructed by the cut and cover method, which makes the station a rarity as one of the only *tube* stations with nothing but stairs from booking hall to platform level. Décor is similar to that of Wanstead.

Gants Hill was built below a roundabout on the Eastern Avenue with subway entrances on the corners. The most striking feature occurs at the foot of the escalators,

Barkingside This station was built by the Great Eastern in 1903, and is one of the most attractive 'country' stations that are today served by the Underground

at platform level, where the 'Moscow' concourse used for the Metropolitan at King's Cross was again a major inspiration. A lofty hall was constructed between the platforms by overlapping further tubes of different diameters. The platforms were decorated in the same manner as at Wanstead, but it is only in this huge hall that the strip lighting was put to really effective use. Further along the line the tracks reached the surface and the old Great Eastern Railway platforms at Newbury Park. Although these were unchanged, the entrance to the station was altered so that pedestrian access was from an arched roof designed as a gigantic shelter for buses and passengers. The work had been planned by Oliver Hill, and it earned him the Festival of Britain award for architectural merit in 1951.

In May 1948 Barkingside, Fairlop and Hainault were opened to Underground trains. The two former stations were built by the Great Eastern in 1903. They are similar period pieces except that the booking hall of Fairlop is a lot smaller and is set next to the viaduct carrying the tracks. The main building at Barkingside is a long symmetrical one, with the booking hall in the centre surmounted by a small tower. The ceiling inside is particularly attractive, with its latticework of supporting wooden beams. Moving on to the platforms one finds that they are linked by a footbridge and have long canopies supported by GER iron brackets identical to those at Newbury Park. It is interesting to note how many old stations are provided with toilets on the platforms – a feature I am sure would be appreciated today. Barkingside is an altogether charming station. One can sit here on a misty day hearing nothing but birdsong and almost imagine that the peace will only be disturbed by the arrival of a steam train. Those illusions are shattered by the appearance of a standard tube train fresh from its journey under the centre of London.

Hainault formed a terminal station for the Central Line, and retains only one of the old GER platforms. It was reconstructed by the LNER but opened by British Rail's Eastern Region with new island platforms and a plain brick entrance below the railway bridge. It is also used for a Central Line shuttle service to Woodford via

Loughton In preparation for the arrival of tube trains, this station was reconstructed by the LNER, which commissioned J.M. Easton for the design work. It was completed in 1940

Grange Hill, Chigwell and Roding Valley, which began in November 1948. The first two are Great Eastern stations of 1903 similar to Fairlop and Barkingside, though Grange Hill has more modern stairs with a brick booking hall on the bridge at the west end and Chigwell has an old building in the same position. Roding Valley is a simple red-brick station with the platforms linked by a footbridge. The diminutive booking hall is on the north side of the station, which was opened by the LNER in 1936.

On the same day as the Woodford–Hainault service opened the Central Line reached Buckhurst Hill and Loughton. The former had two entrances, one built into a new parade of shops and the other on the opposite side of the tracks. Loughton had been built by the Great Eastern as a replacement for the old Eastern Counties station in 1892, and is a small building fronted by two arched windows and an arched door in the centre in the manner of Barkingside. All work carried out by the LNER in connection with the arrival of tube trains elsewhere had basically been carried out in the LT style, but Loughton station is a departure because it was prepared before the war to the requirements of the main line company. It was commissioned as a replacement for the Great Eastern station of 1865, which itself had superseded the Eastern Counties one of 1856. The new Loughton was designed to have an elongated forecourt by John Murray Easton of Stanley Hall, and Easton & Robertson. Externally it is almost like one of Holden's Sudbury boxes, but it is a steel-framed building surfaced with rebated brown bricks giving a strip effect. The single arched window is made up of glass bricks, and inside its contours are continued in the use of a barrel-vaulted form for the ceiling. The two island platforms on the embankment are reached by stairs and a subway. When Loughton was completed in April 1940 it was intended as a forerunner to the large Central Line programme of extensions with what Harry Holland has described as 'its many new and exciting stations'. In truth, however, the eastern end of the Central relies mainly on older stations, with Loughton as its last real outpost of modern architecture.

In November 1949 the Central Line reached Epping, and London Transport took over the steam-worked, single line push-and-pull service between here and Ongar

Ongar The Great Eastern opened this station in 1865; it now forms the terminus of the Underground's most rural service

Platform at Ongar This is the single platform, which is used by a shuttle service between here and Epping. It has seen little alteration during its long life

(which was not electrified until 1957). Apart from Debden, which was modified in the early 1970s, all the stations were originals dating from 1865. By the time they were opened the Eastern Counties Railway had become part of the Great Eastern, to which they may be attributed. Tube trains operated through Debden and Theydon Bois to Epping, with intermediate stations on the shuttle line at North Weald and Blake Hall (the latter was finally closed in 1981). No great urban development had ever grown here in the past, and it is rather difficult to understand why the Underground thought it could generate something better. From its opening until its closure Blake Hall was the only building in a wide area of fields and marshes, a position it held for 114 years. As evidence of how old these stations are one only has to see the 'VR' postbox set into the outside wall at Epping.

The furthest outpost of the Central Line is at Ongar, which never had more than one platform for passengers. There was no platform canopy and the wall alongside it was originally surmounted by just a row of gas lamps. There was a goods yard and loco shed on the southern side, which was finally removed when British Rail pulled out in April 1966. The approach to the station is down a sloping way from the main road where the end of the line occurs, just before what could have been a road bridge if any further extension had ever been built. The station building itself is a single-storey construction that typifies the rural stations of the mid nineteenth century, with their tall chimneys and sloping tiled roofs. At either end of the booking hall the building extends forwards, with the part nearer the road having an additional floor. At the time of writing the station is only used during peak hours, but public concern has prevented the closing of the line completely (not enough, alas, to save poor Blake Hall). Nevertheless the line is still under threat, as the Metropolitan's Brill Branch was half a century earlier. The final closure of North Weald and Ongar may come, but in the meantime it is nice still to be able to observe such eccentricities on the modern Underground network.

The westward extension of the Central Line was contemporary with the eastward one we have been discussing. To start with, the most important development was the building of White City station and the closure of the bottleneck at Wood Lane in November 1947, just a few months after the new line had reached Hanger Lane, Perivale and Greenford. The new White City station had to be fairly large, for it would need to provide terminus facilities required for crews changing trains as East Finchley had done. The design work was carried out by A.D. McGill, the section architect, with assistance from K.J.H. Seymour. Thomas Bilbow, the architect to the Board, supervised the proceedings. Steel-frame construction was used throughout, with floors and roofs of precast concrete slabs and silver-grey and buff facing

Hanger Lane Brian Lewis' design for the GWR was revived by Dr F.F. Curtis after the war, and was still not completed when the Central Line extension opened in 1947

bricks. The station continued the tradition of using metal casement windows. Roughly contemporary with it is the rebuilt West Acton on the Ealing Broadway branch, where the 'box' of the booking hall was made up of two vertical brick walls sandwiching the windows and ceiling. The feel of this building is, however, more in keeping with the new structures designed for the West Ruislip line by the Great Western Railway.

The West Ruislip extension as detailed in the 1935-40 New Works Programme hit financial trouble in the post-war climate of austerity. Most of the plan was redrafted to take account of the new conditions. The Great Western Railway undertook to rebuild its stations for Underground trains, and the first three stations, at Hanger Lane, Perivale and Greenford, were designed personally by that company's chief architect, Brian Lewis. He was succeeded in this capacity in December 1946 by Dr F.F. Curtis, who not only saw the work through to completion but also (with his assistants) produced designs for the other stations on the line.

Work was begun on the three stations in November 1946, but labour shortages and delays due to bad weather meant that they would not be finished by 30 June 1947, the day appointed for the opening of the line. So that this event could proceed, a temporary public access was constructed within the shells of the new buildings at Greenford and Perivale, made up of parts of curved corrugated iron 'Anderson' air raid shelters. This was not practical at Hanger Lane because of the nature

Greenford The contoured canopy is similar to that of Perivale, as both stations were originally designed by Lewis. The building was not completed until 1948

of the site, so a temporary building was constructed made of steel pipes and breezeblocks covered with white 'Snowcrete' and a corrugated roof. Permanent buildings at the sites were not completed until the second half of 1948.

The station at Hanger Lane does not match the interpretation used at the other two. The booking hall was to be both on the road bridge over the tracks and on a corner site. It consisted, when completed, of a circular booking hall with an extended canopy over the entrance and vertical concrete supports. Smaller supports were to form the window frames for the upper portion, which would need to be strong enough to bear the weight of a shallow reinforced concrete dome used as the roof. Lewis' design had been substantially revised here to take account of new techniques and the availability of materials.

Perivale and Greenford stations sit alongside new railway viaducts, and Lewis' designs were closely adhered to. An interesting feature of both of them is the canopy over the entrance, contoured in the manner of a grand piano lid. The Greenford booking hall curved round towards the viaduct arch, where there was a shaft to the right leading up to platform level. To the left there was a subway leading to the old GWR station of 1904, below and to the north, which ceased to be used in 1963. Only when the station was given a new lick of paint in the late 1970s was this subway entrance finally tiled over. Greenford was unique when built in being the only Underground station with an escalator going *up* to the platforms. The platform canopy is, surprisingly, a corrugated affair supported by girders rather than a modern concrete one. The Central Line here serves an island platform, which is divided by a central bay at the eastern end and served by the British Rail shuttle service to Ealing Broadway.

When the Central finally reached West Ruislip in November 1948 it did not serve any new stations but merely the old wooden or red-brick GWR ones. Their rebuilding to Curtis' plans had been postponed through shortage of finance, and progress was made only slowly during the 1950s to complete the programme, though new platforms and buildings with curving concrete canopies had been ready in 1948. Ruislip Gardens was never completed to Curtis' plans. He had proposed a station to the south of the railway viaduct which would resemble a Sudbury box with extended wings on either side forming bus shelters and shops. The only windows in the box would be vertical ones in the side elevations. Nothing was done on the site until the 1960s, by which time the original plans were long outdated. The building that was eventually constructed is far smaller, a tiny booking hall with narrow clerestory windows surrounded by little blocks faced in brick or vertical grey slabs.

At Northolt, South Ruislip and West Ruislip Curtis' designs survived intact with minor modifications. The Northolt booking hall was to be on a bridge at an angle of about 60 degrees to the line, and would

Northolt This station was rebuilt when financial constraints eased, although it adheres closely to Dr F.F. Curtis' original design proposed in 1946

West Ruislip This station building was constructed under the same conditions as Northolt, and forms the western terminus of the Central Line, which reached here in 1948

have a roughly square plan set in a straight line with the platforms. The entrance, however, would be parallel to the road, resulting in an odd appearance for the projecting booking hall walls. The hall was originally supposed to be higher than it was built, with a series of vertical glass panes forming the windows in relief instead of the large horizontal ones that were installed flush with the new walls. The wide entrance planned was narrowed to allow shop accommodation, and the station was rendered in sandy yellow brick with dark brick walls on either side.

South Ruislip was constructed during 1960. Here Curtis' plan had been to use a construction similar to that at Hanger Lane, with a round booking hall with a higher ceiling to form a drum towering over the railway bridge next to it. Under the original scheme the vertical roof supports around the edge would have had recessed windows, each made up of twelve individual vertical panes, but this was abandoned in favour of glass 'walls' each consisting of seven horizontal panes. This configuration overlapped the supports and hid them. Inside the booking hall, below the windows, was a band made up of random plaster reliefs which conceal the fluorescent lighting. West Ruislip corresponds most closely to the Curtis designs. It was faced with the same sandy-coloured bricks as Northolt, but the booking hall windows above the entrance canopy are arranged with vertical panes in the manner that Curtis had intended to employ at his other stations.

With the opening of the eastern and western Central Line extensions the great period of expansion programmes came to an end. The District and Metropolitan had pushed out into suburbia soon after they were built, and the great programmes to unify and extend the system since the First World War had resulted in all the tube lines 'sprouting' at both ends. (This, of course, was with the exception of the Bakerloo, still the only tube railway to retain its original southern terminus at Elephant & Castle.)

With nationalization the London Passenger Transport Board was replaced in 1948 by the London Transport Executive. The last of the old Underground men, Lord Ashfield, had stepped down in October during the previous year and the new Executive began to seek different ways of establishing spending priorities. It at once began to reorganize the road transport system. From its inception in 1933 the LPTB had begun a policy to replace its tram network with trolleybuses. The war had halted this changeover in mid flow; the new body decided that the road fleet should be standardized, and halted purchase of trolleybuses while ordering new motor buses to replace the remaining trams.

So began a period of inactivity unparalleled in the history of the Underground. Work was carried out if and when funds became available, including repairs necessitated by war damage. One of the worst casualties had been Sloane Square station, which had received a direct hit on 12 November 1940 just eight months after being rebuilt with new escalators. The old elliptical roof was destroyed along with the station building, but the Westbourne sewer, which flows in a conduit across the platforms, was not breached. A new prefabricated entrance and platform canopies were brought into use in May 1951. Several other stations sustained war damage and there had also been loss of life, for the platform tunnels were used as air-raid shelters. The underground concourse of the Central Line at Bank was destroyed by a bomb on 11 January 1941, which caused extensive damage and killed fifty-six people. The old District Railway station at Blackfriars was also badly hit.

On a happier note were the minor works carried out at Waterloo and Charing Cross (now Embankment) for the Festival of Britain in 1951. The new décor used at the latter showed the way ahead, and consisted of eggshell blue tiles on the platform supports, with buff for the walls and false ceilings for the canopies, design work being carried out by Jack Howe. The platform indicators were of a new design with plain smoked glass, developed by the LTE signal engineers. The cluttered appearance of the 1920s was swept away with redesigned platform shops in wax-polished wood with sycamore edging.

Major rebuilding works were very few and far between, but the most important in the 1950s was the connection of the District and Central stations at Notting Hill Gate. The old stations had been on different sides of the road, and these were demolished when the new subsurface booking hall and connecting passages, decorated with grey square tiles, finally opened in 1959.

The 1967 resiting of Tower Hill involved different considerations. The new station was situated east of the old one on the site of the Metropolitan's Tower of London station, which had been in use only from 1882 to 1884. Some of the foundations of the adjacent Roman wall were incorporated in the platforms as a feature, and an extra platform was provided to enable District trains to use this as a terminus instead of Mansion House. The booking hall is part of a modern office block – 'Tower House' on the hill opposite the Tower itself.

Another reconstruction which should be mentioned is that at Moor Park, where the Watford and Amersham branches of the Metropolitan meet. In connection with the quadrupling of the line a simple

Barking This huge building was opened by British Rail in 1961, and forms an important link between main line services and the District Line

OXFORD CIRCUS

Booking hall The new booking hall was originally built with extensive provisions for automatic ticket control. Automatic entry and exit gates, controlled by the ticket, were initially a feature of the Victoria Line. Subsequently, however, the exit gates were taken out of service after they were found to be troublesome

Old station entrances The old Oxford Circus station buildings of the Central London Railway (1900) and the Bakerloo (1906) still stand. Their old combined booking hall, beneath Argyll Street, dates from 1925

The Victoria Line provided an opportunity to carry out major reconstruction work at King's Cross, Euston and Oxford Circus. It was largely the pace of work at the last named that dictated progress on the line. The old combined Central/Bakerloo station was already severely congested, and in the new scheme a booking hall, escalators and passages would need to be constructed.

The new booking hall was built directly beneath the Regent Street–Oxford Street junction, and traffic was carried over this on a steel-decked 'umbrella'. This umbrella was installed over the August Bank Holiday in 1963, and was to be a familiar sight in London for nearly five years until its removal over the Easter weekend of 1968.

Entry to Oxford Circus station is by new subway entrances at each corner of the Circus, with additional access via the old Central and Bakerloo buildings and their sub-surface concourse. In peak times even the new station is packed to capacity, making it the second most

used station on the Underground. In 1981 43 million passenger journeys either started or ended here, a figure only exceeded by the 48 million at Victoria. Oxford Circus is equipped with fourteen escalators – more than any other station – and a complicated network of connecting passages in order to speed up two-way passenger flow. With the exception of the Central Line platforms, almost all the station was redecorated for the Victoria Line.

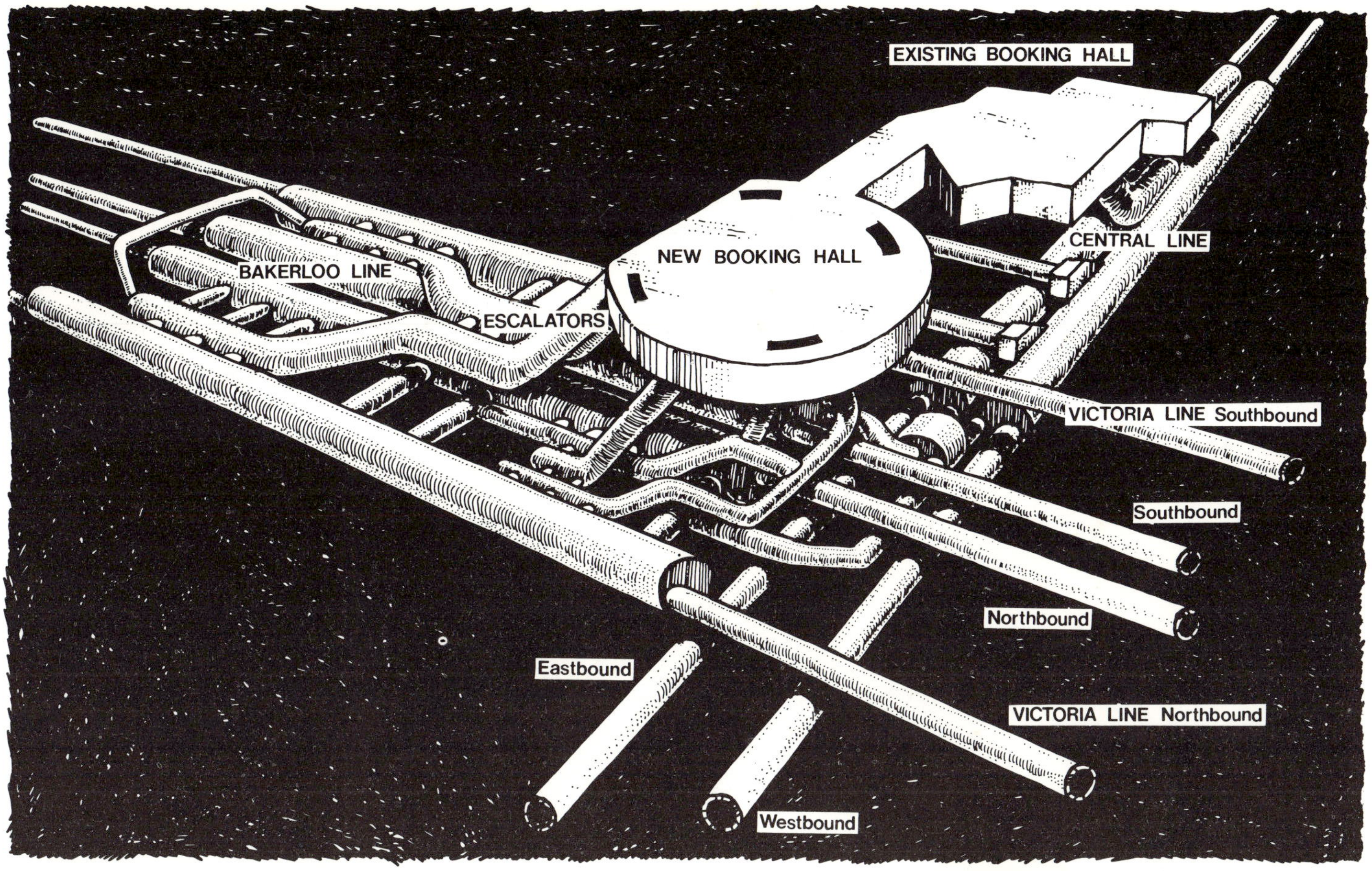

Simplified diagram of Oxford Circus One of the most important aspects considered when planning the Victoria Line was that of cross-platform interchange, effected here by running the Bakerloo Line tunnels between the Victoria. They are linked to the Central Line, which runs at right-angles below them

Victoria Line platform The uniform adoption of square grey tiling throughout the Victoria Line is generally considered to have been a mistake, although panels with separate images were provided at each station. At Oxford Circus an abstract design symbolizes the meeting of the three tube lines

Blackhorse Road This is the only entirely new station building on the northern end of the Victoria Line. It was designed by K.J.H. Seymour and opened in 1968

brick station was built here, with new platforms and access from either side of the line via a subway. It was completed in April 1961.

Not so simple was the new British Rail station used by the District at Barking, which was opened the following September. The main station building is a huge glass-fronted block set back from a forecourt. It is strange that, despite the major building work involved, the platforms were not really altered and retain their old canopies.

The 1960s saw the building of the first new tube railway under London for over half a century. The route that was finally decided upon for the Victoria Line was based on a number of proposals which had been put forward over twenty years before. The idea of the line was to provide a new north–south link connecting many existing stations, principally King's Cross and Victoria. When the first stage to Victoria was opened between September 1968 and March 1969 only one station – Blackhorse Road – did not have interchange facilities with British Rail or other Underground lines.

The initial plans for the stations were announced in 1962 and were the work of K.J.H. Seymour who, it will be recalled, had assisted with the design of White City. Seymour was now chief architect to the Executive and work was begun under his direction. Blackhorse Road was described by John R. Day in *The Story of the Victoria Line*, published on the opening of the line by London Transport, as 'an attractive essay in modern station design'. It featured the most substantial surface building on the line. The spacious booking hall made extensive use of brushed steel, and was rendered externally with dark brown bricks above granite-faced precast concrete panels. The structure was necessarily built around a steel frame, and a band of clerestory windows exposed the rows of fluorescent lights inside. A whimsical concession was the recessed panel near the corner, with a black horse on a mosaic panel.

The surface works at Tottenham Hale, Seven Sisters, Finsbury Park and Highbury & Islington were minor by comparison. Tottenham Hale, for example, has subway and main entrances next to the old British Rail station for which it now provides the entry point, and the Seven Sisters entrance is just a long subway next to the British Rail viaduct. There were no new surface structures at Finsbury Park, and the new works at Highbury took place on the forecourt of the BR station.

The most extensive station work occurred where the new line met the other tubes, from King's Cross southwards. Complicated engineering was required to include new platforms and booking facilities in the existing stations at King's Cross, Euston, Warren Street, Oxford Circus, Green Park and Victoria. At King's Cross the platforms had to be placed on a level between the Circle/Metropolitan platforms of 1941 and the Piccadilly Line, resulting in a combined station on five levels. At the top was the main line station, below which were the Circle, Victoria, Piccadilly and Northern Lines. Old lines were diverted at each station to accommodate the Victoria, but the requirements of cross-platform interchange for trains travelling in the same direction presented some interesting problems at Euston, where the Northern Line's City branch was still using an island platform constructed in 1907 and modernized in the early 1920s. It would have been impossible to place the Victoria Line tunnels between those of the City branch without constructing a new tunnel for northbound trains. The old southbound tunnel was retained and the 'island' extended to the far wall by filling in the old northbound tracks. This has resulted in a very odd-looking 'tube' platform, twice the size of a normal one and with a spare tunnel disappearing at its southern end next to the running tunnel.

Of all the station reconstruction work, that which was carried out at Oxford Circus was the most complicated. The old Central and Bakerloo booking halls were to become redundant, as a large new hall was built under the Circus itself. A huge steel 'umbrella' was constructed to carry road traffic while building work went on beneath. Green Park received a reconstructed booking hall and entrance, and at Victoria a new booking hall was provided just below the surface. To facilitate this it was possible to excavate the forecourt, between the District and main line stations, and when work was completed the new road surface became a large bus station with new shelters and approaches. All of the Victoria Line is in tube tunnel, so all platforms would present a similar appearance.

Aldwych station on the Piccadilly Line has a spare platform, as the other is used only for a shuttle service. This platform has proved very useful to London Transport's designers, enabling full-size mock-ups for proposed decoration schemes to be constructed. The experiments here for the Victoria Line took a year, and resulted in the adoption of a scheme of square grey tiling, a false tunnel ceiling (following the shape of the tunnel roof) and backlit LT roundels with the station name. Concealed lighting would also be used for some advertising display panels; seats, moulded from a hard laminate, would be placed in recesses along the platform wall. Litter bins occupied smaller recesses and the asphalt platform surface, which had been adopted since the late 1930s, was abandoned in a return to paving. The fine art contribution was to form the only difference in the platforms of different stations; each seat recess featured tile designs forming motifs appropriate to this particular station. Particularly effective are Julia Black's Walthamstow Central, which used a complicated floral pattern in the style of William Morris, who lived nearby, and Tom Eckersley's Finsbury Park (crossed duelling pistols), King's Cross (a cross of crowns) and Euston (the old Doric arch that had been demolished in 1962 in advance of the new building programme).

The southern section of the Victoria Line was opened from Victoria to Brixton in July 1971. As with the first stage, only one station, Pimlico (completed the following year), had no connection with another line. The station was built entirely below ground, with a dull grey slab subway entrance. Vauxhall was also below ground, excavated and then covered, with connections to the British Rail station via subways. South of here the line met up with the Northern Line at Stockwell, where the old City & South London station was entirely rebuilt with a single-storey, flat-faced entrance next to a dark brick ventilation tower. Incidentally, the décor used at all stations through which the Victoria Line passed was extended throughout all passageways and connecting tunnels, though in most cases it stopped short of the existing platforms of other lines. Brixton, where a link with BR was planned, received a bright and spacious booking hall with access from a new entrance cut into a row of shops.

The opening of the Victoria Line seems a suitable place to halt before bringing the story up to date. The reader may have noticed, however, that there has been little mention of Walthamstow Central, the northern terminus of the new line. This has been saved to provide a contrast with the more modern aspects of the Victoria Line. True, there was some rebuilding to form a new entrance from the bus stand on the north side of the station, but since all the Victoria's 'treasures' are otherwise below ground access has been provided from the British Rail platforms only. The Victoria is therefore still served by the booking hall on the south side, which was the main entrance to the old station. This was nearly a hundred years old, having been built by the Great Eastern in 1870. It is rather amusing that a building like this could become associated with what was then the most modern underground railway in the world.

Stockwell When the Victoria Line reached the original terminus of the former City & South London tube at Stockwell in 1971, the station had been entirely rebuilt

6 Recent Developments and the Future

The 1970s saw the continuation of works at individual stations along with two major projects, namely the extension of the Piccadilly Line to Heathrow Airport, west of London, and the construction of the Fleet Line (which was renamed Jubilee in the Queen's Silver Jubilee year, 1977). Minor improvement projects were carried out at many stations in and out of town, and some new stations were constructed at old sites.

One of the first projects was carried out at the old London, Tilbury & Southend station at Bromley, which had been renamed Bromley-by-Bow in 1967. The station had been used by District Line trains since 1902 until a serious fire damaged the main entrance on 20 February 1970. An additional entrance was brought into use until British Rail's Eastern Region could open a replacement. This was completed in June 1972, a sturdy little building with a low offset tower and a raised booking hall with clerestory windows. Dark bricks were used for the external facings, in the manner of the most recent Underground designs on the Victoria Line.

The old District Line platforms on the southern side of the Circle Line had already been involved in a lengthening programme for some time by 1968, and the work begun at Cannon Street that year involved correcting an existing stagger by lengthening both platforms in opposite directions. From this relatively minor alteration grew the almost total reconstruction of the station, in association with the building of a tower block over the main line station and a road widening project for Cannon Street itself. The original District building of 1884 was demolished, and sub-surface alterations were carried out in stages by excavating the road and carrying road traffic above on Bailey bridges. The mid-1970s work was completed so that one entrance was used for both the British Rail booking hall and the District one beneath. The tower block was added above these. The new walls on the District platforms were then finished in square beige tiles.

The Barbican development, which has only recently been completed, occupies an area of the City that sustained severe bomb damage during the war. The ambitious plan to redevelop the area included a huge residential complex with an arts centre. This affected the existing Metropolitan and Widened Lines (BR) route between Moorgate and Barbican, and an agreement was reached with the City Corporation to build a new covered way above which the new building work could take place. By the time the project was completed a new entrance to Moorgate station had been built. This has a low entrance with a brown granite facing, the restructured platforms being completely covered over and finished with greyish pink tiling.

The Northern Line to Finsbury Park, which was operated over the Great Northern & City tube of 1904, was transferred to British Rail in September 1975. Just seven months earlier, on 28 February, the line saw the worst accident in the history of the Underground when a Northern Line train ran through the terminal platform and crashed in a dead-end tunnel. Forty-six people were killed. As a result of the disaster many new safety measures were incorporated at terminal stations, including the lengthening of such tunnels to avoid any repetition of this tragic event. North of Moorgate, at Old Street, a road widening scheme meant the demolition of the City & South London/Great Northern & City surface building. A new roundabout was constructed at the junction of City Road and Old Street, and the existing sub-surface booking hall was enlarged to accommodate modern equipment, access being from subway entrances on the corners of the diamond-shaped roundabout which was completed in the early 1970s. The massive ventilation complex in the middle of this roundabout is the only surface feature of the new station.

Other projects in town occurred with the installation of new escalators at several stations. Work at Waterloo during the previous decade involved the opening of a new entrance into the base of the Shell Centre while the old entrance opposite was rebuilt and the original ticket windows and lifts were taken out of use. The project at South Kensington was begun in March 1971, and was mainly concerned with the installation of escalators to replace the lifts in the old Piccadilly station next to the main booking hall. When work was completed the station had been spruced up generally, with new miniature 'gardens' on the District platforms. The now combined booking hall was redecorated and the north retaining wall above the disused District terminal platform was later cleaned to show what the brickwork of the original stations looked like when they were opened in the 1860s. The Piccadilly station building was then used to house ventilation equipment, with the old windows being removed and replaced by wire mesh. To the north of London the station at Archway was reconstructed to be included in a new tower block – Archway Tower – in a similar way to Tower Hill or Lancaster Gate; the latter had been rebuilt in the base of the Royal Lancaster Hotel.

The rebuilding programme on the Uxbridge line in the 1930s had left Ruislip and Hillingdon stations largely unaltered, though the approach to Hillingdon from the road was modified, and the old halts at Ickenham and West Harrow of 1905 and 1913 respectively still survived. Only at Ickenham was any work carried out in the early 1970s, the old wooden booking office on the road bridge being replaced by a modest little building of brick with horizontal white-painted timber.

These brief examples show how much work since the war had been carried out on a piecemeal basis. Only the building of the Victoria Line had resulted in a concerted effort on new works for more than one related station. The extension of the Piccadilly Line to Heathrow was to prove very significant in the modern history of London Transport design, even though only two new stations were planned. Plans had been floated for some time to link up either the BR Southern Region station at Feltham or the Piccadilly Line at Hounslow West with Heathrow Airport. The latter was only two miles from the airport boundary, and a 3½ mile extension would take Underground trains right into the heart of the airport, making London the first major city in the world to have a direct rail link with its main airport. Parliamentary powers for the line were granted in 1967, but it was not until November 1970 that the Underground link option was decided upon. The plan involved an intermediate bus and rail interchange at Hatton Cross on the outskirts of the airport, which could serve not only airport workers but was also in a suitable position to be linked by travolator to a proposed fourth terminal on the southern side of the airport. There was also provision in the plan for a further extension past Heathrow Central, assuming a 'U' shape which could sweep round to a new Terminal Four station, thus making this the terminus should the need arise.

The construction of the extension

Bromley-by-Bow This building was opened by British Rail's Eastern Region in 1972 after a serious fire had caused extensive damage two years earlier

FEATURES OF THE HEATHROW EXTENSION

Hatton Cross exterior Hatton Cross bus and Underground station is a striking solution for the requirements of the site. A necessity was the inclusion of special sound insulation (helped by the design of the entrance), for the station would otherwise be plagued by aircraft noise

The Piccadilly Line reached the centre of Heathrow Airport in December 1977, making London the first city in the world to have a direct urban rail link with its major airport. It was the first project for several years to offer so much scope to the planners, and the opportunity of designing two stations from scratch was seized upon immediately. Hatton Cross (the intermediate station between Hounslow West and Heathrow Central) was built on a spacious corner site, offering the space to experiment with surface building architecture. It opened in 1975, followed two years later by the present terminus of the line.

Heathrow Central presented design problems not unfamiliar in the history of the Underground. Space was at a premium, and the station needed to be below the surface, like so many of those in central London. Sydney Hardy attempted to design an exemplary station within these constraints, and largely abandoned much of the design philosophy that had held sway during the construction of the Victoria Line. The general use of cut-and-cover construction dictated the shape of platforms and sub-surface connections to a great extent, but the ingenious arrangements, which in retrospect appear so simple and obvious, resulted in two stations for which the architecture and design surpassed the standards of the Victoria Line. This approach would be carried a stage further for the construction of the Jubilee Line.

Heathrow Central exterior This entrance houses escalators and is the only surface feature of the station. Most of the passengers enter the station on the moving walkways installed between the booking hall and the terminals

Booking hall, Heathrow Central The incorporation of the illuminated journey planner and exchange facilities into this hall, which occupies a sunken 'box', were essential to the station. Segregation of passengers going to and from London is achieved by streaming in different parts of the concourse

Platform, Heathrow Central The escalators descend right down to the island platform in two shafts – one for 'up' and one for 'down'. The clean platform design is very marked

Ickenham The former Metropolitan Railway halt was replaced by this new booking office in 1971. There are stories of hauntings at this station

was mainly carried out next to the A4 Great West Road and the A30. Much of it was managed using the time-honoured cut-and-cover method rather than driving deep-level tubes, and at one point next to the A30 the trains pop up and run alongside the road before diving underground again on their way to Hatton Cross. The opportunities arose at both Hatton Cross and Heathrow Central of building custom stations, not just adapting existing ones as had for so long been the usual way of updating the system. At Hatton Cross it was also possible to have the main part of the station above ground, although building space for the terminus within the airport itself was as scarce as if the new station had been in the City.

The Hatton Cross Bus and Underground station was completed in July 1975, and its appearance was a total departure from the dark brick uniformity of the Victoria Line works. The clean buff tiles of the exterior walls are topped by a somewhat chunky extended canopy, the sides of which are sculpted and moulded into a relief. Two sides (those facing the main road and the bus forecourt) provide access to the inside through large self-opening glass doors. On entering, one finds that the booking hall itself lies further within, through another set of doors, so that this outer chamber can be used for those waiting for buses. The booking hall itself is clean, spacious and well lit, with a row of ticket windows along one side and a row of entry gates and passimeters (the latter moulded from fibreglass) stretched across the hall. Continuing through, one need only descend the wide, short stairway to the platform level. The cut-and-cover method typically produces an oblong-section trench which is then covered over, so the tracks run only just below the surface. The familiar curved walls of a platform tunnel are therefore absent here, and there is one very wide island platform broken up only by seating and the square pillars supporting the ceiling and building above. These pillars are faced with small mosaic-like tiles, forming a simple motif associated with the station – the 'speedbird' symbol of the old Imperial Airways Company.

The platforms at Heathrow Central are necessarily deeper than those at Hatton Cross, for above them is the main concourse containing the booking hall. As most of the traffic would come directly from the three terminals, all roughly equidistant from the station, the British Airports Authority undertook to build underground travolator links to each one. As a consequence the surface appearance of Heathrow Central is only a simple but very attractive subway entrance connected to the main hall by escalators. The hall is a reinforced concrete structure clad in brick with aluminium louvres above, and was designed to allow further building on top in the future. The main concourse is an oblong concrete box which was built within a huge excavation, afterwards covered over. The internal decoration was carried out mainly with melamine and tiling. Apart from the moulded green passimeters the station also features a bank and a computerized journey planner, which displays in colour the best route to any other Underground station. Two banks of escalators are connected directly to the island platform beneath, which is wider than that of Hatton Cross. A gently curved beige and white suspended melamine ceiling with built-in strip lighting separates the platform line from the tracks, while the concrete pillars are covered in vertical orange tiles. Above the recessed seats is a mural designed by Tom Eckersley (who had worked on murals for the Victoria Line) depicting a silhouette of the Concorde aircraft, and the station name roundels are, of course, illuminated from behind. The station conveys a bright atmosphere with its practical design aspects. By the time it opened in December 1977 the old platforms at Charles Holden's Hounslow West had also been replaced with a new island platform to bring the station up to the standard of Hatton Cross and Heathrow Central. This new section was joined to the old booking hall by a covered walkway.

The man chiefly responsible for the high quality of design on the Heathrow extension was Sydney Hardy, who had just become chief architect to the London Transport Executive. He was to create quite a stir in the late 1970s as he brought in a 'new wave' of designers and architects with the intention of improving design standards. Before we can consider this properly, however, we must turn to the Jubilee Line scheme, which was completed in May 1979.

The Jubilee Line had started life as the Fleet Line, named after the underground river. Its construction was proposed for two main reasons: first, to relieve the heavily congested central section of the Bakerloo (as the Victoria had done for the Piccadilly), and second, to provide a Tube link with docklands. The Bakerloo's Stanmore branch would be transferred to the new line, which would then run south in new tunnels from Baker Street to Bond Street, Green Park, Trafalgar Square/Strand, and on to the City via Aldwych, Ludgate Circus, Cannon Street/Monument, Fenchurch Street and thence to Surrey Docks and the East London section of the Metropolitan. Other schemes suggested a route via Wapping and Millwall as far as Thamesmead. The precise details were left in abeyance when work on the first stage, the Bakerloo relief section, was begun at Bond Street in September 1971. By the following August the contractors were ready to begin the main work of reconstruction here, with the erection of a steel 'umbrella' on part of Oxford Street like that used at Oxford Circus for the building of the Victoria Line. A similar decking was erected in 1973 on the forecourt of the main line Charing Cross station so that work could begin here on the Jubilee's first southern terminus. It was planned that the Bakerloo's Trafalgar Square station should be combined with the Northern Line's Strand, to form a new 'Charing Cross'. The District's Charing Cross station was renamed 'Embankment' to avoid confusion.

Although the running tunnels between Baker Street and Charing Cross were completed by the end of 1974, work on the stations was progressing slowly, despite the fact that north of Baker Street the only reconstruction work involved the 1960s entrances to Swiss Cottage, one of which had a tall grey brick ventilation tower. Seeing that the momentum of construction Bond

Swiss Cottage subway entrance
Almost the only surface alteration to existing stations for the Jubilee Line was this tower added to a subway entrance to the sub-surface booking hall at Swiss Cottage, contemporary with Victoria Line work

BOND STREET

Street station was opened in 1900 by the Central London Railway. Despite alterations in the 1920s it continued to serve only the one tube railway until construction work on the Jubilee Line began, to link the new line and the Central, with a new booking hall.

The use of steel 'umbrella' decking to carry road traffic while new sub-surface booking halls were built had become familiar during the progress of the Victoria Line works at Oxford Circus in the 1960s. In 1972 Oxford Street received its second construction of this type so that the work of converting the station to handle the additional Jubilee Line traffic could be carried out.

When the Jubilee Line opened in May 1979 reconstruction was complete. The station could be entered from three points: a subway entrance on the north side of Oxford Street on the corner of James Street, a subway entrance built into a building on the south side of Oxford Street, and via escalators from the 'West One' shopping centre which was constructed next to it at the same time. The interior décor of the station incorporated extensive use of plastics and tiling, but some features, such as the passimeters, were relics from the 1960s. The station design was not as radical as the conversion work at Charing Cross would eventually prove to be, but nonetheless the clever link with the shopping centre is a major boon at Bond Street.

Shopping arcade entrance On entering the West One shopping centre one can descend in comfort via escalator to the booking hall

Main subway entrance The relatively modest sign above a flight of stairs marks the main street entrance to Bond Street station. A similar entrance to the new Charing Cross was constructed

Booking hall The ticket windows are arranged at one side of the hall. At the barrier the passimeters, used by ticket collectors, are of a standard framed construction with dark melamine-faced chipboard panels

Intermediate concourse Deep-level connections on the Jubilee Line appear far more spacious than their Victoria Line predecessors, an impression heightened by the colourful tiling (in this case, yellow) used instead of uniform light grey

CHARING CROSS

Booking hall The ticket office is moulded in bright green and the fibreglass passimeters are yellow. An interesting effect of spaciousness was created with the abandonment of the plain suspended ceiling in favour of vertical slats and bands with fluorescent lighting

The most major undertaking that the Jubilee Line demanded was the conversion of Strand and Trafalgar Square stations to form a new Charing Cross. Work on stage two – the Bakerloo – was completed in early 1984, but most of the important reconstruction, providing accommodation for the Jubilee and Northern Lines and access to the Bakerloo, was completed when the Jubilee opened in 1979. Despite the original plan to continue the new line to the City and beyond, it now seems that for the foreseeable future Charing Cross will form the southern terminus of the Jubilee.

The sub-surface booking hall at Charing Cross is reached from a large tiled passageway (an attractive haunt for busking string quartets) connected to various subway entrances and the main line station. The rusty-brown tiles used outside the station proper have proved a unifying factor, contrasting sharply with the bright array of colour and inventive design in the booking hall. The Jubilee platforms are separated by a large concourse, befitting the station's importance, which is reached by separate 'up' and 'down' banks of escalators at each end.

The redecoration of the Northern Line platforms with David Gentleman's mural is part of the current philosophy that involves giving stations an individual identity. Gentleman's designs were enlarged and screen-printed on to large panels, which have fortunately been kept free of graffiti. It is now policy to use such materials as melamine and other wipe-clean surfaces at stations to render them vandal resistant.

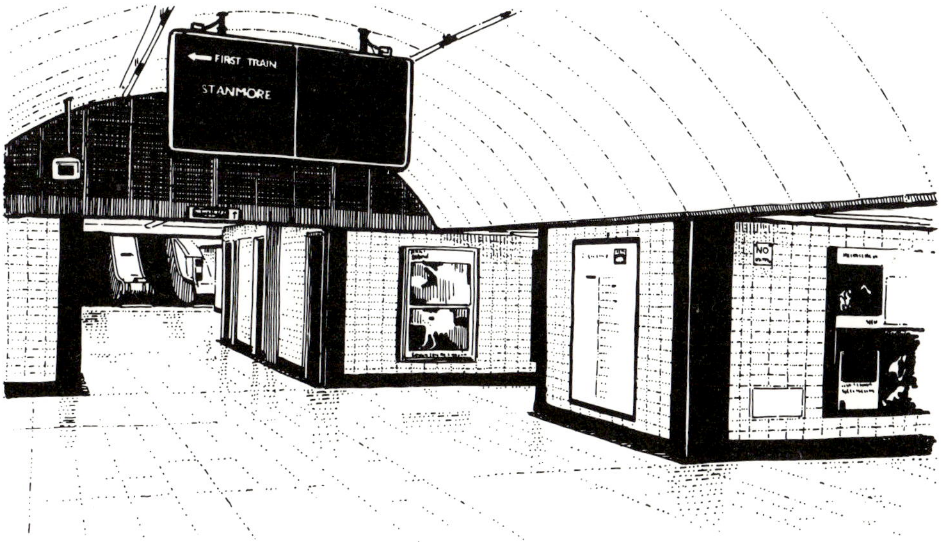

Lower concourse As a terminal station, Charing Cross needs equal access to both Jubilee platforms. This is provided by extending the escalators down to a concourse between the platform tunnels, for the first train out could be leaving from either

Jubilee Line platform Both the overall colour schemes and the platform motifs are sharply varied between Jubilee Line stations. At Charing Cross the platforms are adorned with enlarged photographs of Nelson's Column

Northern Line platform David Gentleman's mural depicts the building of the original 'Eleanor Cross', and incorporates provision in the design for the station name roundel and litter bins. By painting the tunnel ceiling in a dark colour the platform wall has been emphasized

needed to be maintained, London Transport repeated its appeals to the controlling authority, the Greater London Council, and the Government to decide the route of the second stage and to provide financial backing for it. Repeated delays meant that work was not to be started on the line, and the tunnel gangs and engineers who had worked on the first stage fragmented. Attention was instead concentrated on preparing the line as far as Charing Cross, which was planned to open in 1977.

Although work at Baker Street, Bond Street and Green Park was finished when the opening finally went ahead in 1979, work continued through to 1983 at Charing Cross. The conversion of Strand station had formed phase one of the operation, and once this was ready it was possible to route Bakerloo passengers through the new booking hall here while work began on the conversion of the old Trafalgar Square booking hall. The completion of the Baker Street section has, for the moment, resulted in both the 'newest' (Jubilee) and 'oldest' (Metropolitan/Circle) platforms being at this one station.

Jubilee Line platforms differ quite markedly from those of the Victoria Line. In fact they even differ from each other, thanks to a rethink in design policy under Hardy. Instead of standard paving slabs, new light-coloured glazed flooring was used. This had two effects: it helped to reflect light and also to make the grooves at the edge of the platform stand out. The backlit roundel was redesigned to fit snugly into plain plastic panels, instead of illuminating the whole panel as had been done on the Victoria. One area that came in for special attention was the platform ceiling. It was recognized that it was aesthetically more pleasing to break up a continuous bland surface with bands across the ceiling. This was something that Leslie Green had realized seventy years earlier when instead of opting for a platform tunnel faced entirely in uniform white glazed tiles he had consciously done something about breaking up the space. Although his basic layout at each station was the same, the entire colour scheme and pattern had been varied, with bands of the coloured tiles stretching intermittently across the ceiling. Holden had played down this emphasis at his underground platforms, first with the standard decoration scheme and then with his own biscuit-coloured tiling. By the time the Victoria Line platforms were built the only interruptions to the ceiling were accidental ones where the curved panels of the suspended ceiling met.

The Jubilee Line provided another opportunity to incorporate a total design strategy into the platforms. All wiring, signalling equipment and so on was neatly stowed away behind the nameband, which stood proud of the tunnel wall and flush with panels below,

Jubilee Line platform at Baker Street
The platform designs for the Jubilee Line were a great improvement on those of the Victoria Line, completed some ten years previously

which were interspersed with the wall's natural curvature. Each station's individuality was heightened by the use of large panels at various points along the wall; at Baker Street, for example, these show a series of illustrations by Robin Jacques depicting the Adventures of Sherlock Holmes, whereas Charing Cross has enlarged photographs of Nelson's statue. Bond Street has a large parcel made up of tiles, while Green Park's motif is a leaf print. Linear strips made up the ceiling, which had built-in speaker grills and curved bands inserted to emphasize the tunnel shape. Another feature that also began to reappear was the use of different total colour schemes between stations.

The new sense of design spread rapidly to new works outside the Jubilee programme. At Harrow-on-the-Hill an extended entrance in College Road was opened in 1981. Above it was a faceted, light brick office building that could provide shelter for passengers walking from the railway station to the new bus station. This is a long, smoked-glass, single-storey construction with self-opening doors, each of which forms a bus stop for a particular route or routes. New bus garages at Hackney, Westbourne Park and Plumstead were opened in the same year and also reflect the new spirit. The booking hall at West Ham also received a facelift. It is a small hall, under the railway bridge carrying the original London, Tilbury & Southend Railway platforms now used by the District. A new entrance door was fitted, and inside a bright colour scheme in

Harrow-on-the-Hill The new extended entrance to this station was opened in 1981 in association with the adjacent bus station

Lift at Wapping This automatic lift, with its audible and visual warning signals, is typical of the type currently being installed at Underground stations where escalators are impractical

yellow, green and blue was introduced along with the installation of melamine, brushed steel and glass fibre fittings.

New projects on the engineering side have absorbed a lot of funds, particularly in the replacement of antiquated lifts at many stations. Wherever possible automatic lifts are being installed, as at Earl's Court (brought into use in 1982). Hampstead station, the deepest on the system with shafts descending 181 feet, was in 1982 in the unique position of having three generations of lifts–two original Otis lifts dating from 1907, two high-speed lifts installed about thirty years later, and two brand new automatic high-speed installations. Standard lifts only operate at 180 feet per minute, but high-speed ones can travel at up to 800 feet per minute. At Hampstead there is a warning notice advising passengers not to use the emergency stairs down to the platforms, as there are over three hundred steps in the descent! Work at Wapping resulted in a rebuilt booking hall in 1982, which housed two of the new lifts. Each has illuminated warnings to 'stand clear of the doors', while also emitting an audible signal as well.

By the late 1970s there were two main batches of old stations badly in need of a facelift. Before dealing with the East London section of the Metropolitan we should consider the dilapidated state of the original Central London Railway stations used by the Central Line between Shepherd's Bush and the City. These were largely ignored during various redecoration programmes and fell into a state of disrepair which surpassed that of Leslie Green's stations for the Underground Group of six or seven years later. The latter became *the* typical early tube stations and the CLR's were to a large extent forgotten for nearly eighty years. Of course there were alterations to booking halls and layouts, but the platforms were rarely changed and by the end of the 1970s were in rather poor shape. A plan was proposed to redecorate them along with some of the Bakerloo platforms. The first to be completed were those of the Bakerloo at Baker Street, and they showed a change in direction from the decorative schemes used on the Jubilee Line. The platform surface remained the same but instead of costly panelling on the curved wall and ceiling a new tiling scheme was adopted. New brown tile bands stretched over the tunnel ceiling and a distinctive motif of a silhouette of Sherlock Holmes, made up of thousands of little silhouettes glazed on to tiles, was employed all along the platforms. All extraneous cables were grouped together in a brown aluminium duct running the length of the platform and bearing the station name at intervals.

The importance of emphasizing the individuality of a station had been most markedly demonstrated by the murals on the Northern Line at Charing Cross, which David Gentleman designed to run the whole length of the platforms and were lit by concealed lighting

Bakerloo Line platform at Baker Street The conduit is a feature of modern Underground platform design, but the Sherlock Holmes motifs are exclusive to Baker Street

Central Line platform This platform at Tottenham Court Road is one of three initial platform decoration schemes at some of the most heavily used Central Line stations

above. The Central Line project involved thirteen stations with the new approach, which was as follows. First, each station needs a corporate image, identifying it symbolically with the rest of the Underground; second, each has to have a line identity. This can mainly be achieved by the use of a repeated colour appropriate to the line at each location. Last, the stations should have their own identity emphasized in whatever way is possible. The Central project established a 'kit of parts' that could be used to fulfil the first two criteria at minimal cost, while individual agencies were invited to submit ideas for the image of each station.

The 'kit' consisted of a red duct like those used at Baker Street, raised up to emphasize the exits with thin tubes running across the ceiling. By using this method it was hoped to create the maximum effect for the least cost, as the old tunnel walls would not need to be panelled over. New seats, litter bins and other items were designed to form part of the kit and experiments were carried out at the disused Aldwych platform, which had seen many previous such attempts at new approaches. The tubes could be used to support poster panels and seats as well as routes for any future rewiring, and it was hoped that the haphazard clutter along the walls existing at present would not be repeated. By avoiding false ceilings and plastic panels money could also be redirected to other parts of each station, for it was estimated that such installations would cost less than a quarter of those on the Victoria Line. In any case all the expenditure in making each station on that line look the same was by now regarded as having been a big mistake.

The brief for designers for both Baker Street modernization and the updating of the Central Line was basically to retain what was good or historic, but to remove piecemeal additions while respecting and expanding on each station's character. During 1979 and early 1980 a series of highly inventive proposals was put forward for the Central Line. Holland Park, for example, would have a tree planted in the booking hall with a colour scheme of greens throughout the station to echo the foliage (a plan later modified to replace the tree with plant troughs). The station buildings and platforms would have a substantial fine art input with commissioned murals from leading artists. Among the interesting proposals for decoration at platform level was a design at Marble Arch related to Speaker's Corner, although it was replaced by the Arch itself in later designs. Queensway would have a nightlife theme. Colours would be based around purple and blue with yellow at the exits and violet filters on the lights; the scheme led to Queensway being dubbed 'the first "punk" station'. The architectural newspaper *Building Design* reported on the new proposals on 11 January 1980, but on 22 February, under a heading 'LT Cuts Hit Architects' came the news that the design consultants had been told to stop work. The newspaper went on to say that financial restrictions had meant the postponement or abandoning of most of the project, and that morale within the architecture department was 'at an all-time low'. There was a fear that Sydney Hardy's team would be disbanded, but work on three of the stations – at Bond Street, Oxford Circus and Tottenham Court Road – is continuing in modified form at the time of writing under Hardy's successor, D.W.C. Hall. For the time being at least a responsible and inventive department is continuing to further good design, and this part of London Transport has now become the Department of Architecture *and* Design.

With restricted budgets it is never easy to refurbish an old line like the East London section. One of the first signs of a project here was the erection of new beige panels along the platforms to hide the plain brickwork. This was a technique employed many years before at several older stations on the Circle Line, but these new melamine panels were a great improvement on the old clutter of painted wooden panels such as those at Notting Hill Gate, Bayswater and Paddington. The work at Wapping has been mentioned, and in January 1983 the refurbishing of three other stations was completed. Two new escalators and a flight of stairs were opened in a shaft between an intermediate landing and the shell of the old booking hall at Rotherhithe. This shaft is covered by curved glass, and is the only one of its kind on the system. The booking hall interior was rebuilt, and finished in brown and beige panelling of either melamine or enamelled metal. The old booking hall at Shadwell was closed and a new one opened on a new site. This is faced with dark brown bricks and has a distinctive angled wall/ceiling of tinted glass with light green edging. When viewed from the front it in fact looks like a large greenhouse. The platform access at the end of the station was rebuilt with the installation of new automatic lifts like those at Wapping.

The largest new surface building on the Underground at the time of writing is the new booking hall at Surrey Docks. This is built on an acutely angled corner between Lower Road and Rotherhithe Old Road, more or less in line with the running tracks below. A small shop was built into the apex of the new building, which is stepped back to allow the insertion of the hall itself. This has access from two sides, with the Lower Road entrance being the largest. The whole intricate structure is faced in light-coloured bricks and is well in keeping with the

Shadwell This distinctive new booking hall was opened in January 1983 as part of the attempt to brighten up the old East London section of the Metropolitan

design spirit of London Transport in the 1980s. There has indeed been a 'renaissance' in London Transport architecture and design in recent years, since the low period that followed the departure of Frank Pick and Charles Holden. This has been combined with a growing awareness of its architectural heritage – in 1981 the London Transport Museum mounted an exhibition of London Transport Architecture.

On 10 January 1983, exactly 120 years after the opening of the Metropolitan Railway, work began on the old Metropolitan/Circle platforms at Baker Street to restore them to their original Victorian style. This work involves cleaning up the brickwork and renewing ceramic tiles in the shafts along each platform. Before the station was built over, sunlight would flood down these shafts, and new sodium lights are to be placed in each of them to recreate this effect. Most modern traces, such as fluorescent lighting, are to be removed, and new platform seats in the original style will be installed in the recesses.

What plans are there for the immediate future? It is hoped that work on the Central and East London will continue, financial restraints permitting. The Greater London Council, which runs London Transport, was involved in a series of legal problems over subsidies, and a long-term stable policy that would allow further rationalization of the system has yet to take effect. In Paris in the early 1970s a high level of subsidy was decided upon which resulted in that city now having the most up-to-date urban transport system in the world.

It could be argued that projects nowadays are subject to the most frustrating delays caused by bureaucracy. Certainly Watkin, Forbes, Yerkes, Ashfield and Pick would not have been put off the further development of the Jubilee Line. But perhaps those days were easier – or those men knew instinctively that something was viable. For the present, it seems that phase two of the Jubilee Line has been abandoned, the main proposal to serve docklands now being a Light Rapid Transit Railway. Whether this would, strictly speaking, be part of the Underground has still to be decided. It is currently proposed that the scheme should be finished by the mid-1980s and should run from a site near Tower Hill along existing underused or disused British Rail viaducts to the Isle of Dogs. The only large station will be

Surrey Docks The largest new surface building on the system to date is the one at Surrey Docks, which exemplifies the current architectural spirit

Escalators at Rotherhithe These escalators were brought into use early in 1983, and the melamine panelling is a departure from the brushed steel previously used. The enclosed glass canopy is unique on the system

Kensal Green This pleasant booking hall is the most recent architectural addition made to the system by British Rail, and demonstrates an approach different from London Transport solutions

at Minories, next to the viaduct into Fenchurch Street. Passengers could here change to the main system at Tower Hill. Other stations are likely to be little more than platforms with shelters, and may even be built by parties outside London Transport's direct control. Apart from the Executive the project involves the Greater London Council, the London Docklands Development Corporation, and the property developers themselves. At present final details for the line are still to be worked out.

There are, however, other projects under immediate consideration, including a massive programme at Liverpool Street and the Terminal Four station on the Piccadilly Line. It was announced in January 1983 that the extension to the new terminal currently under construction should be completed by 1985. The work at Charing Cross has at last been completed, and one can certainly detect a return of the philosophy of Pick and Holden here. Mike Emerson, the project architect, states his objects as attracting passengers by making the station as pleasant as possible '. . . also to improve the environment from the passenger point of view, to make his journey through our system that much more enjoyable, something to relate to, some interest, even provoking comment'. Comment is something that there ought to be, for there is over 120 years of history of architecture and design involved in London's Underground stations. Nobody can predict future trends, but in the *T.O.T.* staff magazine for November 1931 was an article entitled 'The Underground in 2031'. I would not like to say how accurate the whimsical drawing of a future station reproduced here is, but probably only the predicted date is wrong. After all, Heathrow Central was opened in 1977 . . .

Morden – a cartoon depicting 'The Underground in 2031' Published in *Train, Omnibus, Tram* (staff magazine) in 1931

APPENDIX: LOGOS AND MOTIFS

The Underground system of the 1980s bears many reminders of its long history. Throughout the network are distinctive features which can be attributed to particular companies, logos used either as decorative features or as functional characteristics. The use of Metropolitan and District Railway motifs was widespread up to the early years of this century, and the other railway companies also used corporate symbols at their stations. Many can still be seen today, on stations built by the Underground companies and on those taken over by the Underground. The four on this page are examples of the kind of feature to be found.

GER The Great Eastern logo is incorporated here into a canopy bracket at Newbury Park

LTSR This canopy bracket at Bromley-by-Bow is an example of those used by the London, Tilbury & Southend Railway

DR This is a District Railway symbol in the booking hall at the rebuilt Fulham Broadway station

MR Wembley Park features this device on its exterior, indicating 'Metropolitan Railway 1923'

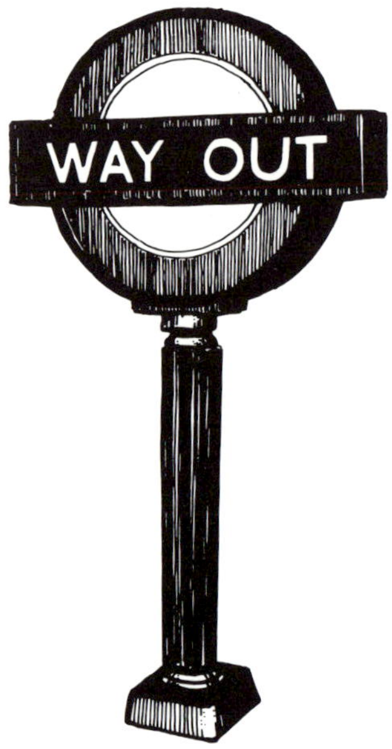

'Way Out' sign at Swiss Cottage

Bibliography and List of Sources

Books

Barker, T.C./Robbins, M. *A History of London Transport Vol. 2* (Allen & Unwin 1976)
Barman, Christian *The Man Who Built London Transport* (David & Charles 1979)
Betjeman, John/Gray, John *London's Historic Railway Stations* (John Murray 1972)
Biddle, Gordon/Spence, Geoffrey *The British Railway Station* (David & Charles 1977)
Briggs, M.S. *Building To-Day* (Oxford University Press 1944)
Borley, H.V. *Chronology of London Railways* (Railway & Canal Historical Society 1982)
Course, Edwin *Railways Then and Now* (Batsford 1979)
Day, John R. *The Story of the Victoria Line* (London Transport 1970)
—— *The Story of London's Underground* (London Transport 1979)
Edwards, Dennis/Pigram, Ron *Metro Memories* (Midas Books 1977)
—— *The Final Link* (Midas Books 1982)
Follenfant, H.G. *Reconstructing London's Underground* (London Transport 1974)
Freeborn, J./Duncalf, L./Green, O. *Time Travel Trail* (London Transport Museum 1982)
Green, Andrew *Our Haunted Kingdom* (Wolfe Publishing 1973)
Heaps, Chris *London Transport Railways Album* (Ian Allan 1978)
Holland, H. *Travellers' Architecture* (Harrap & Co. 1971)
Howson, H.F. *London's Underground* (Ian Allan 1981)
Klapper, Charles *London's Lost Railways* (Routledge & Kegan Paul 1976)
Lee, Charles E. *Sixty Years of the Piccadilly* (London Transport 1966)
—— *100 Years of the District* (London Transport 1968)
—— *The Metropolitan Line* (London Transport 1972)
Mitchell, N.G.H./Robins, I.J. *Notes for Visitors to London's Underground* (London Underground Railway Society 1979)
Nock, O.S. *Underground Railways of the World* (A. & C. Black 1973)
Robbins, M. *Baker Street Station* (St Marylebone Society, 24 April 1974)
Rose, Douglas *The London Underground: A Diagrammatic History* (Douglas Rose 1980)
Service, Alastair *The Architects of London* (Architectural Press 1979)
—— *London 1900* (Granada 1979)

Internal Publications and Brochures

Underground Electric Railways of London Ltd – reprinted articles used for publicity:
The Tramway & Railway World: Baker Street & Waterloo Railway (8 March 1906)
—— *Great Northern, Piccadilly & Brompton Railway* (6 December 1906)
Railway Times: Charing Cross, Euston & Hampstead Railway (22 June 1907)
City & South London Railway Extension to King's Cross, St Pancras and Euston (11 May 1907)
LER Brochures:
Golders Green–Hendon Extension (19 November 1923)
Opening of the Hendon–Edgware Extension of the Hampstead Line (18 August 1924)
Opening of the Morden Extension and the Kennington Loop (September 1926)
A Note on Contemporary Architecture in Northern Europe – Pick/Holden/Edwards (1931)
Operating Manager's Personal Letter No. 11 (30 March 1931)
Underground to Heathrow (London Transport 1977)

Periodicals

The Architect Vol. 124 No. 11, November 1978, pp. 19-25: 'End of the Line' by Colin Davis
Architects' Journal Vol. 95, 26 March 1942: Frank Pick Obituary
—— Vol. 114, 9 August 1951, p. 161: 'Improvements for the Festival of Britain'
—— Vol. 136, 29 August 1962, p. 523: 'Proposals for Victoria Line Stations'
Architectural Association Quarterly Vol. 8, No. 2, 1976, pp. 28-39: 'Charles Holden and his London Underground Stations' by Grahame Middleton
Architectural Review February 1940, pp. 49-50: 'St John's Wood'
—— August 1942, pp. 31-48: 'Patient Progress' the life work of Frank Pick by Nikolaus Pevsner
—— December 1975: 'Singing the Body Electric with Charles Holden' Hanson
—— February 1980, pp. 124-5: 'London Underground Modernisation'
Arkitekten September 1932, pp. 153-76: 'Study of London's Underground Stations'
The Builder Vol. 175, 16 July 1948, pp. 66-72: 'Architectural Work on the Central Line'
—— Vol. 178, 12 May 1950, pp. 632-5: 'White City Station'
Building Design No. 245, 11 April 1975, pp. 12-13: 'Underground Architect' by Martin Mayer
—— No. 478, 11 January 1980, pp. 18-19: 'Central Line Proposals' by Dayan Sudjic
—— No. 484, 22 February 1980, p. 1: 'LT Cuts Hit Architects'
Designer Extra November 1980: Christian Barman Obituary by Enid Marx
Pennyfare (staff magazine) February 1934: 'The Southgate Extension'
Railway Gazette Supplement 18 November 1932: 'Underground Extensions & Improvements'
—— 1946: 'Improving London's Transport' in chapter 5, pp. 81-6, 'Stations & Buildings'
Railway Magazine April 1961, pp. 282-3: 'Architecture in Transport' by Dr F.F.C. Curtis
—— February 1963, pp. 93-102: 'The Metropolitan in its Prime' by Charles E. Lee
RIBA Journal Vol. 15, 1908, p. 621: Leslie Green Obituary
TOT (staff magazine) November 1931, pp. 367-8: 'The Underground in 2031'

Broadcasts

The London Underground Open University Course 'History of Architecture & Design 1890-1939' by Dr Geoffrey Baker
The London Programme 12 November 1982, London Weekend Television

Index to Stations

The names given are current in 1983; former station names appear in brackets.
Station opening dates refer to services of the Underground or its predecessors.
Stations built by other companies are credited in the 'remarks' column, which also lists major alterations to stations. References in inverted commas refer to the commencement or ceasing of Underground services at an existing station. Page numbers given in *italics* refer to illustrations in text, numbers in parentheses refer to features.

	OPENED	REMARKS	PAGE
Acton Town (Mill Hill Park 1879–1910)	1879	Reconstructed 1910, 1932	15, 29, 76–7, *77*, 79
Aldgate	1876	Reconstructed 1927	14, 17
Aldgate East	1884	Resited 1938	18, 27, 91
Aldwych (Strand 1907–15)	1907	Closed between 1940–6	42, 46, 113, 119, 127
Alperton (Perivale-Alperton 1903–10)	1903	Reconstructed 1931	24, 74, 76, 77
Amersham (Amersham & Chesham Bois 1922–34)	1892		22
Angel	1901	Closed for alterations 1922–4	36, 58, *59*
Archway (Highgate 1907–39) (Archway (Highgate) 1939–41) (Highgate (Archway) 1941–7)	1907	Additional entrance 1912 New entrance 1977	46, 97, 98, 115
Arnos Grove	1932		78, 79, 80, 82, *82*
Arsenal (Gillespie Road 1906–32)	1906		46
Aylesbury (I)	1892	Closed 1894	22
Aylesbury (II)	'1894'	Opened by Great Western 1863, reconstructed 1908, 1926; 'Closed 1961'	22, 91
Baker Street (Metropolitan) ('Bakerloo') (Jubilee)	1863 1906 1979	Extended 1868, rebuilt 1911–28, stations combined 1940; Bakerloo building later demolished	7, 8, *8*, 23, 29, (30–1), 33, 43, 46, 93, 119, 124, *124*, 125, 126–7, *126*, 129
Balham	1926		58
Bank ('Northern') ('Central')	1900 1900	Linked to Waterloo & City (built 1898); altered 1925; reconstructed 1946 (war damage)	35–6, *35*, 37, 40, 41, 67, *67*
Barbican (Aldersgate Street 1865–1910) (Aldersgate 1910–23) (Aldersgate & Barbican 1923–68)	1865	Roof demolished, alterations 1955	8–9, 10, 114
Barking	'1902'	Opened by L.T.&S. 1854, altered 1906–8; reconstructed 1961	28, 88, *109*, 112
Barkingside	'1948'	Opened by Great Eastern 1903	*102*, 103, 104
Baron's Court	1905		*24*, 27, 46, 47
Bayswater (Bayswater (Queen's Road) & Westbourne Grove 1923–33)	1868		9, 9, *11*, 12, 13, 32, 128
Becontree (Gale Street 1926–32)	'1932'	Opened by L.M.S. 1926, rebuilt 1932	88
Belsize Park	1907		46
Bethnal Green	1946		99
Blackfriars	1870	Superstructure destroyed 1940	*13*, 14, 109
Blackhorse Road	1968		112, *112*
Blake Hall	'1949'	Opened by Great Eastern 1865; closed 1981	105
Bond Street	1900	Reconstructed 1920s, 1979	37, 40, *40*, 58, 67, 119, (120–1), 124, 125, 128
Borough	1890	Closed for alterations 1922–5	33, 35
Boston Manor (Boston Road 1883–1911)	1833	Reconstructed 1934	19, *83*, 84
Bounds Green	1932		78, 79
Bow Road	'1902'	Opened by Whitechapel & Bow 1902	*27*, 28
Brent Cross (Brent 1923–76)	1923		52–3
Brill	'1899'	Opened by Wotton Tramway 1872; closed 1935	23, 91
British Museum	1900	Closed 1933	37, *38*, 40–1, 67
Brixton	1971		113
Bromley-by-Bow (Bromley 1894–1967)	'1902'	Opened by London, Tilbury & Southend 1894; various alterations; rebuilt 1972	28, 114, *115*, *131*
Brompton Road	1906	Closed 1934	46, 91
Buckhurst Hill	'1948'	Opened by Eastern Counties 1856; main reconstruction 1892	104
Burnt Oak	1924		53, *53*
Bushey (Bushey & Oxhey 1912–75)	'1917'	Opened by London & Birmingham 1841, reconstructed 1897; 'closed 1982'	49
Caledonian Road	1906		46

	OPENED	REMARKS	PAGE
Camden Town	1907		46, 54, 58
Cannon Street	1884	Reconstructed between 1968–75	17, 114, 119
Canons Park (Canons Park (Edgware) 1932–3)	1932		70, 71
Carpenders Park	'1919'	Opened by L.& N.W. 1914; resited 1952; 'closed 1982'	49, 90
Castle Hill (Ealing Dean)	'1883'	Opened by Great Western 1871; 'closed 1885'	19
Chalfont & Latimer (Chalfont Road 1889–1915)	1889		19, 22
Chalk Farm	1907		46
Chancery Lane	1900	Altered 1934	37, 40, 67
Charing Cross ('Northern'–Charing Cross (Strand) 1914–15) (Strand 1915–73) ('Bakerloo'–Trafalgar Square 1906–79) (Jubilee)	1907 1906 1979	Strand closed 1973, re-opened 1979 after reconstruction; linked to former Trafalgar Square and new Jubilee Line	33, 43, 46, 119, (122–3), 124, 126, 127, 130
Chesham	1889		*17*, 19, 22
Chigwell	'1948'	Opened by Great Eastern 1903	104
Chiswick Park (Acton Green 1879–87) (Chiswick Park & Acton Green 1887–1910)	1879	Reconstructed 1932	15, 77, *78*, 84
Chorleywood (Chorley Wood 1884–1915) (Chorley Wood & Chenies 1915–34) (Chorley Wood 1934–65)	1889		19
City Road	1901	Closed 1922	36, 91
Clapham Common	1900	Closed for alterations 1923–4	36, 58
Clapham North (Clapham Road 1900–26)	1900	Closed for alterations 1923–4	36, 58
Clapham South	1926		58, 68
Cockfosters	1933		79, 82, 85, 86
Colindale	1924	Entrance later altered	53
Collier's Wood	1926		59
Covent Garden	1907		6, (44–5), 46
Croxley (Croxley Green 1925–49)	1925		69–70, *70*, 71
Dagenham East (Dagenham 1885–1949)	'1902'	Opened by London, Tilbury & Southend 1885; reconstructed 1932	28, 88–9, *88*
Dagenham Heathway (Heathway 1932–49)	1932		88
Debden (Chigwell Road, April–Dec. 1865) (Chigwell Lane 1865–1949)	'1949'	Opened by Great Eastern 1865; Entrance altered c. 1972	105
Dollis Hill	1909	Reconstructed 1939	25, 96
Down Street	1907	Closed 1932	46, 67, 91
Drayton Park	1904	'Closed 1978'	36
Ealing Broadway (District) ('Central')	1879 '1920'	District station later rebuilt; Central used Great Western (1838) station, known as Ealing until 1875; new combined B.R., Central & District entrance opened 1966	15, *23*, 26, 50, 51, *51*, 88, 107
Ealing Common (Ealing Common & West Acton 1886–1910)	1879	Reconstructed 1931	15, 24, 68, 89
Earl's Court	1871	Resited 1878; altered c. 1905, 1937	14, 16, (20–1), 26, 27, 46, 47, 61, 126
East Acton	1920		50, *50*
Eastcote	1906	Reconstructed 1939	25, 84, 85
East Finchley	1939	Built on site of former Edgware, Highgate & London station (1867)	(94–5), 97, 105
East Ham	'1902'	Opened by London, Tilbury & Southend 1858; reconstructed 1902	28
East Putney	1889		22
Edgware	1924		53–4, *54*, 61, 86, 97
Edgware Road (Metropolitan)	1863	Altered c. 1922	7, 8, 10, 12, 32
Edgware Road ('Bakerloo')	1907		43, 47
Elephant & Castle ('Northern') ('Bakerloo')	1890 1906	'Northern' entrance closed for alterations 1923–4; reconstructed again 1970s	33, 35, 43, 50, 108
Elm Park	1935		89
Embankment (District–Charing Cross 1870–1974) (District) ('Bakerloo') (Others – Charing Cross (Embankment) 1914–15) (Charing Cross 1915–74) (Charing Cross Embankment 1974–76) ('Northern')	1870 1906 1914	Stations combined during major reconstruction 1926–8	14, 43, (56–7), 58, 109

	OPENED	REMARKS	PAGE
Epping	'1949'	Opened by Great Eastern 1865	104–5
Essex Road (Canonbury & Essex Road 1922–48)	1904	'Closed 1975'	36
Euston ('City Branch')	1907	Originally two separate stations linked with the main line; both later demolished; major reconstruction 1968	36, 37, *37*, 46, 58, 110, 112–3
('Charing X Branch')	1907		
(Victoria)	1968		
Euston Square (Gower Street 1863–1909)	1863	Entrance reconstructed 1931	7, 8, 67
Fairlop	'1948'	Opened by Great Eastern 1903	103, 104
Farringdon (Farringdon Street 1863–1922) (Farringdon & High Holborn 1922–36)	1863	Resited 1865 Entrance altered 1922	7, 8, 9, 32, *32*
Finchley Central	'1940'	Opened by Edgware, Highgate & London as Finchley & Hendon (1867)	97, 98
Finchley Road	1879	Reconstructed 1913, 1939	16, 93, 96
Finsbury Park (Great Northern)	1904		46, 112, 113, 114
('Piccadilly')	1906		
('Victoria')	1968		
Fulham Broadway (Walham Green 1880–1952)	1880	Entrance later altered	16, 25–6, *131*
Gants Hill	1947		101, 102–3
Gloucester Road (District) (Brompton (Gloucester Road) 1868–1907)	1868		9, 12, *12*, 25
Gloucester Road ('Piccadilly')	1907		46, 47
Golders Green	1907		46, 47, 52
Goldhawk Road	1914		15
Goodge Street (Tottenham Court Road 1907–8)	1907		46, 47
Granborough Road (Grandborough Road 1868–1920)	'1894'	Opened by Aylesbury & Buckingham 1868; closed 1936	22
Grange Hill	'1948'	Opened by Great Eastern 1903	104
Great Missenden	1892	'Closed 1961'	22
Great Portland Street (Portland Road 1863–1917) (Great Portland Street & Regent's Park 1923–33)	1863	Entrance reconstructed c. 1920	7, 8, 29, *32*
Greenford	1947		105, 106–7, *106*
Green Park (Dover Street 1906–33)	1906	Reconstructed 1933, 1969; Further alterations 1979	46, 67, 112, 113, 119, 124, 125
Gunnersbury	'1877'	Opened by L. & S.W. as Brentford Road (1869)	15, 16
Hainault	1948	Reconstructed from former Great Eastern station (1903)	103–4
Hammersmith (Hammersmith & City)	1864	Resited 1868; altered 1939–48	15
Hammersmith (District/Piccadilly)	1874	Rebuilt 1882; alterations c. 1905, 1932	15, 27, 46, 47, 76, 77, 84
Hammersmith (Grove Road)	'1877'	Opened by L. & S.W. (1869); 'closed 1907'	15
Hampstead	1907		46, 47, *47*, 126
Hanger Lane	1947	Work completed 1948	105, 106–7, *106*, 108
Hanwell	'1883'	Great Western station (1838); 'closed 1885'	19
Harlesden	'1917'	Opened by L. & N.W. 1912	49
Harrow & Wealdstone	'1917'	L. & N.W. station of 1897 on site of older one; 'closed 1982'	49, *49*, 50
Harrow-on-the-Hill (Harrow 1880–94)	1880	Reconstructed 1939–48	16, 19, 24, 69, 97, 125, *125*
Hatch End (Pinner & Hatch End 1897–1920) (Hatch End for Pinner 1920–56)	'1917'	L. & N.W. station of 1897 on site of older one; 'closed 1982'	49
Hatton Cross	1975		115, (116–7), 118–9, 130
Hayes & Harlington	'1883'	Great Western station (1864); 'closed 1885'	19
Headstone Lane	'1917'	Opened by L. & N.W. 1913; 'closed 1982'	49
Heathrow Central	1977		115, (116–7), 118–9
Hendon Central	1923		52–3, *52*, 84
High Barnet	'1940'	Opened by Great Northern 1872	*96*, 97–8
Highbury & Islington (Highbury 1904–22)	1904	Victoria Line station (1968) alterations	36, 112
Highgate	1941		98
High Street Kensington	1868	Reconstruction completed 1906	9, 25
Hillingdon	1923		25, 115
Holborn (Holborn (Kingsway) from 1933)	1906	Major alterations 1933	41, 46, 47, 58, 67, 68
Holland Park	1900		37, *39*, 40, *40*, 127
Holloway Road	1906		46, 47

	OPENED	REMARKS	PAGE
Hornchurch	'1902'	Opened by London, Tilbury & Southend 1885; reconstructed 1932	28, 88, 89
Hounslow Central (Heston–Hounslow 1886–1925)	1886	Rebuilt 1912	19, 29, *29*
Hounslow East (Hounslow 1883–4) (Hounslow Town 1884–1925)	1883	Resited 1909 after previous closure 1886–1903	19, 29
Hounslow West (Hounslow Barracks 1884–1925)	1884	Reconstructed 1926–31; interior reconstructed 1975	19, 68, *68*, *69*, 89, 115, 119
Hyde Park Corner	1906	Alterations c. 1930	46, 67
Ickenham	1905	Reconstructed 1971	25, 115, *118*
Kennington	1890	Closed for alterations 1923–5	33, 34, *34*, 35, 36, 54, 58
Kensal Green	1916	Rebuilt c. 1979	49, 50, *130*
Kensington (Olympia) (Kensington (Addison Road) 1868–1946)	'1906'	West London station (1862) on site of previous one	29
Kentish Town	1907		46
Kenton	'1917'	Opened by L. & N.W. 1912; 'closed 1982'	49
Kew Gardens	'1877'	Opened by L. & S.W. 1869	15
Kilburn (Kilburn & Brondesbury 1879–1950)	1879	Alterations 1939	16, 96
Kilburn Park	1915		48, 49
King William Street	1890	Closed 1900	33, 35
Kingsbury	1932		70, *71*
King's Cross St. Pancras (Metropolitan – King's Cross 1863–1925) (Metropolitan) (King's Cross & St. Pancras 1925–33) ('Piccadilly') ('Northern') (Victoria) ('Piccadilly' – King's Cross 1906–27) (King's Cross for St. Pancras 1927–33) ('Northern' – King's Cross for St. Pancras 1907–33)	1863 1906 1907 1968	Major work 1941; further alterations 1968	7, 8, 10, 12, 36, 46, 97, 98, 110, 112, 113
Knightsbridge	1906	Entrance reconstructed 1934	46, 67
Ladbroke Grove (Notting Hill 1864–1880) (Notting Hill & Ladbroke Grove 1880–1919) (Ladbroke Grove (North Kensington) 1919–38)	1864		15
Lambeth North (Kennington Road March–Aug. 1906) (Westminster Bridge Road 1906–17)	1906		43
Lancaster Gate	1900	Entrance reconstructed 1960s	37, 40, 115
Langley	'1883'	Great Western station (1845); 'Closed 1885'	19
Latimer Road	1868		15, 29
Leicester Square	1906	Reconstructed 1930–5	46, 67
Leyton	'1947'	1879 Reconstruction by Great Eastern of older station	100
Leytonstone	'1947'	1892 Reconstruction by Great Eastern of older station; further reconstruction 1947	98, 100
Liverpool Street (I)	Feb. 1875	Closed July 1875	14
Liverpool Street (Bishopsgate 1875–1909) ('Circle') ('Central')	July 1875 1912	Reconstruction c. 1930	14, 18, 41, 98, 130
London Bridge	1900	Closed for alterations 1923–4; Entrance rebuilt 1967	35
Lord's (St. John's Wood Road 1868–1925) (St. John's Wood 1925–1939)	1868	Closed 1939	91
Loughton	'1948'	1865 Great Eastern station on site of older one; reconstructed 1940	98, *103*, 104
Maida Vale	1915		48, *48*, 49
Manor House	1932		78, 79, 82
Mansion House	1871	Entrance reconstructed c. 1930	14, 17, 67
Marble Arch	1900	Reconstructed 1932	37, 67, 127
Marlborough Road	1868	Closed 1939	91
Marylebone (Great Central 1907–17)	1907	Entrance transferred to inside main-line station 1943	43, 47
Mile End	1902	Reconstructed 1946	28, 99
Mill Hill East	'1941'	Formerly Edgware, Highgate & London 'Mill Hill' (1867)	97, 97, 98
Monument (Eastcheap Oct.–Nov. 1884)	1884	Major reconstruction 1935	17, 27–8, 41, 67, 119

		OPENED	REMARKS	PAGE
Moorgate (Metropolitan– Moorgate Street 1865–1924)	(Metropolitan)	1865	Alterations c. 1976	8, 14, 35, 36, *36*, 114
	('Northern')	1900		
Moor Park (Sandy Lodge 1910–23) (Moor Park & Sandy Lodge 1923–50)		1910	Reconstructed 1961	25, 69, 109
Morden		1926		59, 60–1, *60*, *61*, 68, 73, 86, 130, *130*
Mornington Crescent		1907		46
Neasden (Kingsbury & Neasden 1880–1910) (Neasden & Kingsbury 1910–32)		1880	Alterations 1939	16, 91, 96–7
Newbury Park		'1947'	Opened by Great Eastern 1903; alterations 1949	98, 100, 103, *131*
New Cross		'1884'	Opened by South Eastern 1850	18
New Cross Gate (New Cross 1839–1923)		'1884'	Opened by London & Croydon 1839	18
North Acton		1923		50, 98
North Ealing		1903		24, 84
Northfields (Northfield (Ealing) 1908–11) (Northfields & Little Ealing 1911–32)		1908	Resited 1932–3	
North Harrow		1915	Later altered	25
Northolt		'1948'	Reconstructed 1950s	107–8, *107*
North Weald		'1949'	Opened by Great Eastern 1865	105
North Wembley		'1917'	Opened by L. & N.W. 1912; 'closed 1982'	49
Northwick Park (Northwick Park & Kenton 1923–33)		1923		25
Northwood		1887	Reconstructed 1962	19, 71, 97
Northwood Hills		1933		71–2
Notting Hill Gate	('Circle')	1868	Station reconstructed and combined 1960	9, *10*, 37, 109, 128
	('Central')	1900		
Oakwood (Enfield West 1933–4) (Enfield West (Oakwood) 1934–46)		1933		79, 80
Old Street		1901	Closed for alterations 1922–4; reconstructed c. 1975	36, 114
Ongar		'1949'	Opened by Great Eastern 1865	98, *104*, 105, *105*
Osterley (Osterley & Spring Grove 1883–1934)		1883	Resited 1934	19, *83*, 84
Oval (Kennington (Oval) 1890–4)		1890	Closed for alterations 1923–4	33, *33*, 35, 58, *58*
Oxford Circus	('Central')	1900	Combined 1925; reconstructed 1969	37, 40, 43, (110–1), 112, 113, 119, 120, 128
	('Bakerloo')	1906		
	(Victoria)	1969		
Paddington (Paddington (Bishops Road) 1863–1933)	(Metropolitan)	1863		7, 9, 15, 48
	('Bakerloo')	1913		
Paddington (Paddington (Praed Street) 1868–1948)		1868	Alterations c. 1920	9, *10*, 13, 32, 128
Park Royal (Park Royal & Twyford Abbey 1903–31) (Park Royal (Hanger Hill) 1936–47)		1903	Resited 1931; reconstruction completed 1936	24, 84
Parsons Green		1880		16
Perivale		1947		105, 106–7
Piccadilly Circus		1906	Reconstructed 1928	43, *43*, 46, (62–3), 64, 66, 67, 68, 92
Pimlico		1972		113
Pinner		1885		19, 71
Plaistow		'1902'	Opened by London, Tilbury & Southend 1858; reconstructed 1903–5	28
Preston Road		1908	Reconstructed 1931–2	25, 71
Putney Bridge (Putney Bridge & Fulham 1880–1902) (Putney Bridge & Hurlingham 1902–32)		1880		*14*, 16, 18
Quainton Road		'1894'	Opened by Aylesbury & Buckingham 1868, rebuilt 1896; 'closed 1936–43', '1948'	22, 91
Queensbury		1934		70, 71
Queen's Park		'1915'	L. & N.W. station Queen's Park (West Kilburn) 1879; altered 1915, c. 1977	49, 88, 90
Queensway (Queen's Road 1900–46)		1900		37, *39*, 40, 127
Ravenscourt Park (Shaftesbury Road 1873–88)		'1877'	Opened by L. & S.W. 1873	15, 77
Rayners Lane		1906	Reconstructed 1938	25, 29, 84–5, *84*, *85*
Redbridge		1947		101, 102, *102*
Regent's Park		1906		43, 46

	OPENED	REMARKS	PAGE
Richmond	'1877'	Opened by L. & S.W. 1869; reconstructed 1937–8	15, 72, 88, 89, *90*
Rickmansworth	1887		*16*, 19
Roding Valley	'1948'	Opened by LNER 1936	104
Rotherhithe	'1884'	Opened by East London 1869	*15*, 17, 18, 19, 128, *129*
Royal Oak	1871	Altered 1904	15
Ruislip	1904		*19*, 24, 115
Ruislip Gardens	'1948'	Opened by Great Western/Great Central 1934; reconstructed 1960s	107
Ruislip Manor	1912	Closed 1917–19; reconstructed 1938	25, 84
Russell Square	1906		46
St. James's Park (55 Broadway)	1868	Reconstructed 1928–9	13, (64–5), 66, 92, 95
St. John's Wood	1939		82, 91, 93, *93*, 96, 98, 99
St. Mary's (Whitechapel Road) (St. Mary's 1884–1923)	1884	Closed 1938	18, 91
St. Paul's (Post Office 1900–37)	1900	Altered 1929, c. 1939	37, *38*, 40, 67
Seven Sisters	1968		112
Shadwell (Shadwell & St. George in the East 1900–18)	'1884'	Opened by East London 1876; reconstructed entrance 1982–3	17, 128, *128*
Shepherd's Bush (Hammersmith & City)	1864	Resited 1914	15
Shepherd's Bush ('Central')	1900		37, 40, 41, 50, 126
Shoreditch	'1913'	Opened by East London 1876	11, 19
Sloane Square	1868	Rebuilt 1951	10, 13, 109
Slough	'1883'	Opened by Great Western 1840; resited 1884; 'closed 1885'	19
Snaresbrook	'1947'	1893 reconstruction by Great Eastern of older station	100, *100*
South Acton	1905	'Closed 1959'	29
South Ealing	1883	Altered c. 1933	19, 77, 96
South Harrow	1903	Resited 1935	24, 29, 84
South Kensington (District) ('Piccadilly')	1868 1907	Altered c. 1900, 1971–3	9, 10, 13, *23*, 25, 27, 46, 47, 115
South Kentish Town	1907	Closed 1924	46, 91
South Kenton	1933	'Closed 1982'	49
South Ruislip	'1948'	Opened by Great Western/Great Central as 'Northolt Junction' 1908; reconstructed 1961	107–8
South Wimbledon	1926		59
South Woodford (South Woodford (George Lane) 1937–50)	'1947'	Resited by Great Eastern 1883 as George Lane	100–1, *101*
Southall	'1883'	Opened by Great Western 1839, 'closed 1885'	19
Southfields	1889		22
Southgate	1933		79, (80–1), 82–3
Stamford Brook	1912	Additional platform 1932	29, 77
Stanmore	1932		69, 70, 71, *72*, 91
Stepney Green	1902		28
Stockwell	1890	Closed for alterations 1923–4; reconstructed 1971	33, 35, 36, 58, 113, *113*
Stoke Mandeville	1892	'Closed 1961'	22
Stonebridge Park	'1917'	Opened by L. & N.W. 1912	49, 90
Stratford	'1946'	Main reconstruction 1946 on site of Eastern Counties original (1839)	98, 99–100, *99*
Sudbury Hill	1903	Reconstructed 1931–2	24, 74, 76, *76*, 77, 79, 85
Sudbury Town	1903	Reconstructed 1931	24, 69, 73, (74–5), 76, 77, 78, 79
Surrey Docks (Deptford Road 1869–1911)	'1884'	Opened by East London 1869; reconstructed 1982–3	18, 119, 128–9, *129*
Swiss Cottage (Metropolitan)	1868	Closed 1940	91
Swiss Cottage ('Jubilee')	1939	Alterations 1979	91, 93, 96, 98, 119, *119*, *132*
Temple	1870	Reconstructed 1911–2	14, *25*, 27
Theydon Bois	'1949'	Opened by Great Eastern as 'Theydon' 1865; enlarged 1885	105
Tooting Bec (Trinity Road (Tooting Bec) 1926–50)	1926		58, 59, *59*, 60

	OPENED	REMARKS	PAGE
Tooting Broadway	1926		58, 66
Tottenham Court Road ('Central') ('Northern'–Oxford Street 1907–8) ('Northern')	1900 1907	Stations combined c. 1929	37, 40, 41, *41*, 46, 47, *127*, 128
Tottenham Hale	1968		112
Totteridge & Whetstone	'1940'	Opened by Great Northern as 'Totteridge' 1872	97
Tower Hill (Tower of London 1882–4) (Mark Lane 1884–1946)	1882	Resited 1884; rebuilt on original site 1967	17, 18, 109, 115, 129–30
Tufnell Park	1907		46
Turnham Green	'1877'	Opened by L. & S.W. 1869; reconstructed 1911	15, 77
Turnpike Lane	1932		78, *79*, 82, 84
Upminster	'1902'	Opened by London, Tilbury & Southend 1885; reconstructed 1932	28, 88, 89
Upminster Bridge	1934		89, *89*
Upney	1932		88
Upton Park	'1902'	Opened by London, Tilbury & Southend 1877; altered 1903	28, *28*
Uxbridge	1904	Resited 1938	24, 68, 82, 85, (86–7), 94, 96, 97
Uxbridge Road	'1906'	Opened by West London 1869; Closed 1947	29
Vauxhall	1971		113
Verney Junction	'1894'	Opened by L. & N.W./Aylesbury & Buckingham 1868; 'closed 1936'	22, 91
Victoria	1868	Reconstructed c. 1900; alterations 1969	13, 111, 112, 113
Waddesdon (Waddesdon Manor 1897–1922)	1897	Closed 1936	22
Waddesdon Road (Waddesdon 1899–1922)	'1899'	Opened by Wotton Tramway 1872; closed 1935	23
Walthamstow Central	'1968'	Access from Great Eastern 1870/97 station; alterations 1968	113
Wanstead	1947		101, *101*
Wapping	'1884'	Opened by East London as 'Wapping & Shadwell' 1869; alterations 1980	17, 18, 119, *125*, 126, 128
Warren Street (Euston Road 1907–8)	1907	Reconstructed c. 1932; alterations 1968	46, 47, *66*, 67–8, 112
Warwick Avenue	1915		48, 49
Waterloo	1906	Alterations 1926, 1951, 1960s	43, 54, 58, 109, 114
Watford	1925		69, 70, 71
Watford High Street	'1917'	Reconstructed by L. & N.W. 1912 on previous site; 'closed 1982'	49
Watford Junction	'1917'	Originally opened by L. & N.W. 1858; 'closed 1982'	49, 90
Wembley Central (Wembley for Sudbury 1910–48)	'1917'	Originally opened by London & Birmingham c. 1842 as 'Sudbury'; reconstruction completed 1948	49, 89–90, *91*
Wembley Park	1894	Altered 1923, 1931, 1948	69, 71, *131*
Wendover	1892	'Closed 1961'	22
West Acton	1923	Reconstructed c. 1948	50, 106
West Brompton	1869		14
West Drayton	'1883'	Opened by Great Western 1838; resited 1884; 'closed 1885'	19
West Finchley	'1940'	Opened by LNER 1933	97
West Ham (West Ham (Manor Road) 1924–69)	'1902'	Opened by London, Tilbury & Southend 1901; alterations 1981	28, 125
West Hampstead	1879	Reconstructed 1898; alterations 1938	16, 91, 96
West Harrow	1913		*22*, 25, 115
West Kensington (North End (Fulham) 1874–7)	1874		15
West Ruislip	'1948'	Opened as Ruislip & Ickenham by GWR/GCR 1906; reconstructed 1950s	98, 107, 108, *108*
Westbourne Park	1866	Altered 1871	15
Westcott	'1899'	Opened by Wotton Tramway 1872; closed 1935	23
Westminster (Westminster Bridge 1868–1907)	1868	Alterations c. 1900, 1925	12, 13–14, 27, *55*, 58
White City (Hammersmith & City) (Wood Lane 1908–47)	1908	Closed 1959	15

	OPENED	REMARKS	PAGE
White City (Central)	1947		41, 50, 105–6, 112
Whitechapel (Whitechapel (Mile End) 1884–1901)	'1884'	Opened by East London 1876; reconstructed 1902	*11*, 18, *26*, 28
Willesden Green	1879	Reconstructed 1914	16, 32, 96–7
Willesden Junction	'1915'	Opened by L. & N.W. 1912	49
Wimbledon	1889	Reconstructed 1929	22, 72, 88, 89
Wimbledon Park	1889		*18*, 22
Windsor	'1883'	Opened by Great Western 1849; 'Closed 1885'	19
Winslow Road	'1894'	Opened by Aylesbury & Buckingham 1868; closed 1936	22
Wood Green	1932		78, 79
Wood Lane	1908	Closed 1947	41, *42*, 50, 105
Wood Siding	'1899'	Opened by Wotton Tramway 1872; closed 1935	*18*, 23
Woodford	'1947'	Great Eastern 1892 reconstructed on older site	98, 100, 101, 103
Woodside Park	'1940'	Opened as Torrington Park, Woodside by Great Northern 1872	97
Wotton	'1899'	Opened by Wotton Tramway 1872; closed 1935	23
York Road	1906	Closed 1931	46, 91

General Index

Aberconway, Lord 7
Aumonier, Eric 64, 95, 97
Aylesbury & Buckingham Railway 22

Baker Street & Waterloo Railway ('Bakerloo Line') 30, 32, 33, 42, 43, 46, 47, 48–9, 56, 57, 63, 72, 85, 90, 91, 93, 96–7, 108, 110–11, 113, 119, 122, 126
Barlow, Peter William 33
Barman, Christian 46, 78
Betjeman, Sir John 9, 30
Bilbow, Thomas 105
Black, Julia 113
Brompton & Piccadilly Circus Railway 42
Brunel, Isambard Kingdom 17, 51
Brunel, Sir Marc 17, 18, 33
Bucknell, L.H. 85, 86, 94, 97

Central London Railway ('Central Line') 24, 28, 33, 37–41, 42, 47, 50–1, 67, 85, 98–108, 109, 110–11, 113, 120, 126, 127, 129
Charing Cross, Euston & Hampstead Railway ('Hampstead') 41, 42, 46, 47, 52, 54, 56, 58
Circle Line (Inner Circle) 8, 10, 11, 12, 16, 17, 31, 33, 98, 112, 114, 124, 128, 129
City & South London Railway 23, 33–7, 41, 42, 43, 44, 50, 54, 55, 56, 113, 114
City of London & Southwark Subway Company 34, 58
Clark, C.W. 29, 30, 32, 69, 70
Curtis, Dr F.F. 106–8

Dalrymple-Hay, Sir Harley H. 42–3
Day, John R. 112
District Railway (Metropolitan District Railway) 10, 12–19, 20, 22–9, 32, 33, 41, 42, 46, 47, 51, 56, 57, 58, 67, 68, 72, 73, 76–7, 84, 88–9, 91, 99, 108, 109, 112, 113, 114, 115, 125, 131
Dudok 73

Ealing & Shepherd's Bush Railway 50
East London Railway 10, 11, 15, 17, 18, 28
Eastern Counties Railway 98, 99–100, 104, 105
Easton, John Murray 104
Eckersley, Tom 113, 119
Edgware, Highgate & London Railway 95, 97, 98
Emerson, Mike 130
Epstein, Jacob 64, 65, 66

Figgis, T. Phillips 34, 36
Forbes, James Staats 16, 17, 19, 24, 129
Ford, Harry W. 27, 46
Fowler, Sir John 7, 10, 11, 12, 13

Gentleman, David 122, 123, 126
Gibb, Sir George 42, 47, 55
Gill, Eric 64
Great Central Railway 17, 23, 69, 98
Great Eastern Railway 98, 100–1, 102, 103–4, 105, 113, 131
Great Northern Railway 7, 8, 36, 42, 78, 96, 97
Great Northern & City Railway 36, 42, 114
Great Northern & Strand Railway 42
Great Northern, Piccadilly & Brompton Railway 20, 27, 36, 42, 44, 46
Great Western Railway 7, 8, 15, 18, 19, 22, 23, 27, 50–1, 98, 106–7
Greater London Council 124, 129, 130
Greathead, James Henry 33
Green, Leslie W. 20, 24, 37, 43–8, 61, 62, 66, 124, 126
Grenander 73

Hall, D.W.C. 128
Hammersmith & City Railway 15
Hardy, Sydney 116, 119, 128
Harris, 'Bumper' 21
Harrow & Uxbridge Railway 28
Heaps, Stanley 52, 53, 55, 66, 67, 70, 93, 96, 99
Hill, Oliver 103
Holden, Charles 54, 55, 58–60, 62, 64, 66, 67, 68, 72, 73–86, 88, 89, 91–2, 93, 94, 96, 97, 99, 101, 102, 104, 119, 124, 129, 130
Howe, Jack 109

James, C.H. 79
Jacques, Robin 125
Johnston, Edward 55
Joseph, Delissa 37
Jubilee Line 30, 32, 33, 56, 58, 65, 72, 90, 114, 116, 119–25, 126, 129

Lewis, Brian 106–7
London & Birmingham Railway 7, 89
London & North Eastern Railway 69, 78, 96, 97, 98, 99, 100, 103
London & North Western Railway 48–50, 89, 90, 91
London & South Western Railway 15, 16, 18, 22, 29, 72
London, Brighton & South Coast Railway 18
London, Chatham & Dover Railway 16, 17
London Docklands Development Corporation 130
London Electric Railway ('Underground Group') 42, 47, 50, 52, 53, 54, 60, 65, 66, 70, 73
London General Omnibus Company 54
London, Midland & Scottish Railway 88–9, 90, 91

London Passenger Transport Board 52, 55, 71, 79, 108
London, Tilbury & Southend Railway 28, 88, 114, 125, 131
London Transport Executive 108, 109, 112, 119, 130

Manchester, Sheffield & Lincolnshire Railway 17, 22
McGill, A.D. 105
Measures, Harry B. 37, 40
Metropolitan Railway 7–9, 10, 12–19, 22–6, 28, 29, 30–1, 32, 33, 46, 52, 67, 69–72, 73, 82, 85, 86, 90–1, 93, 94, 96–7, 98, 103, 105, 108, 109, 112, 114, 118, 119, 124, 126, 128, 129, 131
Middleton, Grahame 99
Moore, Henry 64

Northern Line 33, 34, 35, 42, 54, 57, 67, 85, 91, 97–8, 112–3, 114, 122, 123, 126

Pearson, Charles 7
Pevsner, Sir Nikolaus 46, 76
Piccadilly Line 15, 21, 24, 27, 29, 33, 41, 42, 47, 63, 67, 68, 73, 76–8, 80, 82, 84–5, 86, 91, 97, 112, 113, 114, 115, 119, 130
Pick, Frank 54–5, 58, 59, 60, 64, 66, 68, 72, 73, 78, 80, 86, 90, 98–9, 129, 130

Seymour, K.J.H. 105, 112
Shaw, Norman 14
Smith, Sidney 37
South Eastern Railway 16, 17, 18, 23, 46
Southern Railway 56, 72, 88, 89, 90
Speyer, Edgar 42
Staal, J.F. 84
Stabler, Harold 79
Stanley, Sir Albert (Lord Ashfield) 47, 55, 90, 98, 99, 108, 129

Underground Electric Railways Company of London Ltd 42–3, 44
Uren, Reginald H. 84

Victoria Line 33, 52, 58, 65, 88, 110–11, 112–13, 114, 115, 116, 118, 119, 121, 124, 127

Waterloo & City Railway 37, 41, 42
Watkin, Sir Edward 16, 17, 18, 19, 22, 23, 24, 129
West London Railway 29
Whitechapel & Bow Railway 26, 27, 28
'Widened Lines' 9
Wotton Tramway 22

Yerkes, Charles Tyson 24, 27, 42, 46, 129

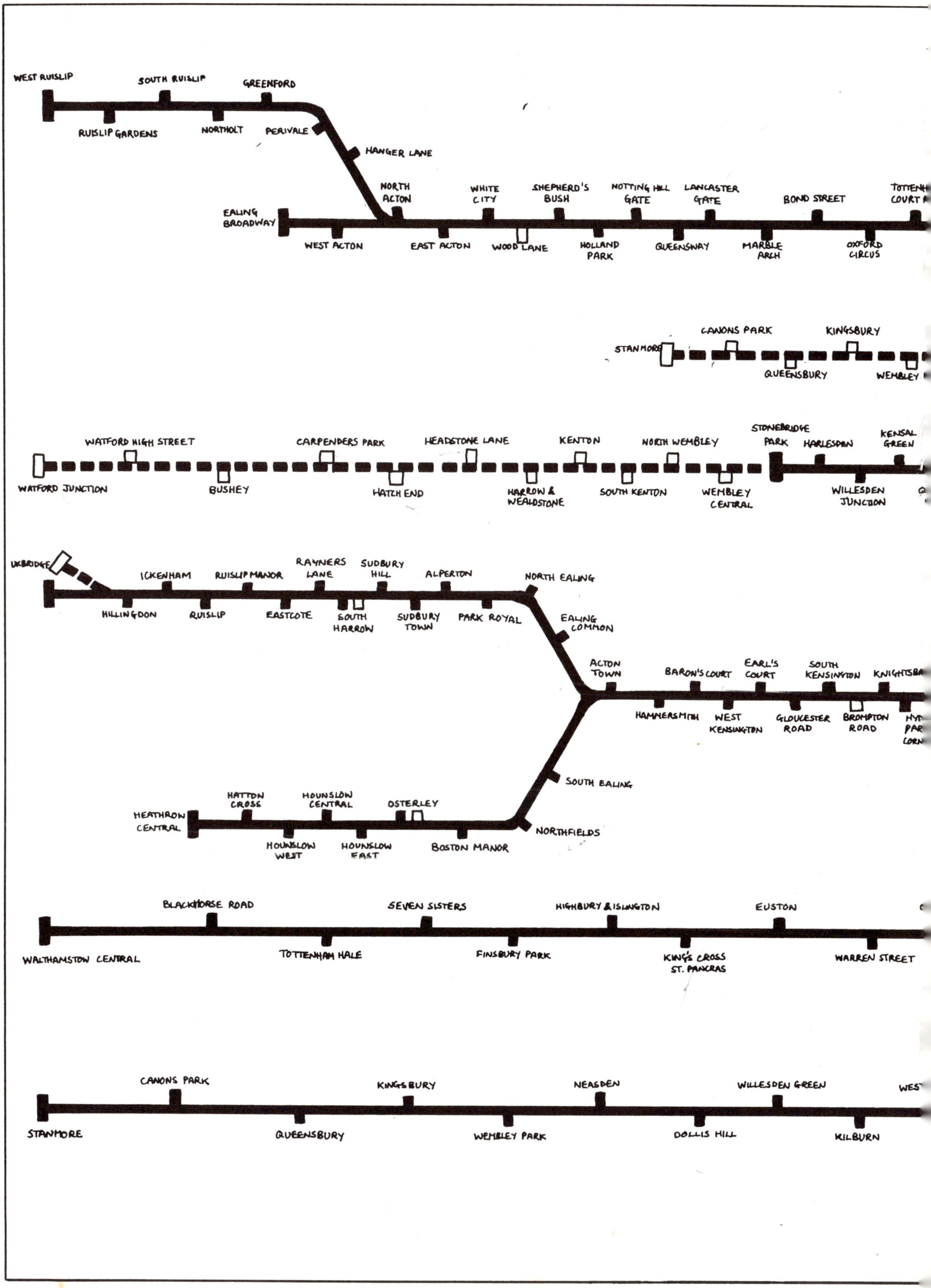
WEST RUISLIP
SOUTH RUISLIP
GREENFORD
RUISLIP GARDENS
NORTHOLT
PERIVALE
HANGER LANE
NORTH ACTON
WHITE CITY
SHEPHERD'S BUSH
NOTTING HILL GATE
LANCASTER GATE
BOND STREET
EALING BROADWAY
WEST ACTON
EAST ACTON
WOOD LANE
HOLLAND PARK
QUEENSWAY
MARBLE ARCH
OXFORD CIRCUS
CANONS PARK
KINGSBURY
STANMORE
QUEENSBURY
WATFORD HIGH STREET
CARPENDERS PARK
HEADSTONE LANE
KENTON
NORTH WEMBLEY
STONEBRIDGE PARK
HARLESDEN
KENSAL GREEN
WATFORD JUNCTION
BUSHEY
HATCH END
HARROW & WEALDSTONE
SOUTH KENTON
WEMBLEY CENTRAL
WILLESDEN JUNCTION
UXBRIDGE
ICKENHAM
RUISLIP MANOR
RAYNERS LANE
SUDBURY HILL
ALPERTON
NORTH EALING
HILLINGDON
RUISLIP
EASTCOTE
SOUTH HARROW
SUDBURY TOWN
PARK ROYAL
EALING COMMON
ACTON TOWN
BARON'S COURT
EARL'S COURT
SOUTH KENSINGTON
HAMMERSMITH
WEST KENSINGTON
GLOUCESTER ROAD
BROMPTON ROAD
SOUTH EALING
HATTON CROSS
HOUNSLOW CENTRAL
OSTERLEY
HEATHROW CENTRAL
HOUNSLOW WEST
HOUNSLOW EAST
BOSTON MANOR
NORTHFIELDS
BLACKHORSE ROAD
SEVEN SISTERS
HIGHBURY & ISLINGTON
EUSTON
WALTHAMSTOW CENTRAL
TOTTENHAM HALE
FINSBURY PARK
KING'S CROSS ST. PANCRAS
WARREN STREET
CANONS PARK
KINGSBURY
NEASDEN
WILLESDEN GREEN
STANMORE
QUEENSBURY
WEMBLEY PARK
DOLLIS HILL
KILBURN